P9-CPZ-783

Science Projects About

Math

Robert Gardner

Enslow Publishers, Inc.

40 Industrial Road	PO Box 38
Box 398	Aldershot
Berkeley Heights, NJ 07922	Hants GU12 6BP
USA	UK

http://www.enslow.com

Library of Congress Cataloging-in-Publication Data

Gardner, Robert, 1929–
    Science projects about math / by Robert Gardner.
       p. cm. — (Science projects)
    Includes bibliographical references and index.
    Summary: Presents projects and experiments suitable for science fairs, utilizing
mathematical skills in relation to light, temperature, angles and heights, distance, time,
and velocity.
    ISBN: 0-89490-950-9
    1. Mathematics—Experiments—Juvenile literature. [1. Mathematics—Experiments.
2. Science—Experiments. 3. Science projects. 4. Experiments.] I. Title. II. Series:
Gardner, Robert, 1929–   Science projects.
QA40.5.G374   1999
507.8—dc21   98-6820
                                                  CIP
                                                       AC

Printed in the United States of America

10 9 8 7 6 5 4 3 2

Illustration Credits: Michelle St. Germain

Cover Photo: Jerry McCrea (foreground); © Corel Corporation (background).

Contents

*appropriate ideas for science fair project

*appropriate ideas for science fair project

Introduction

This book is filled with projects and experiments that make use of mathematics. As you will see, mathematics is a valuable tool for scientists. Most of the materials you will need for performing these experiments can be found in your home or school. Several of the activities may require materials that you can buy in a supermarket, a hobby or toy shop, or a hardware store. You will need someone to help you with the few activities that require more than one pair of hands. It would be best if you work with friends or adults who enjoy experimenting as much as you do. In that way you will both enjoy what you are doing. If any danger is involved in doing an experiment, it will be made known to you. In some cases, to avoid any danger, you will be asked to work with an adult. Please do so. We do not want you to take any chances that could lead to an injury.

Like any good scientist, you will find that it is useful to record in a notebook your ideas, notes, data, and anything else you can conclude from your experiments. By doing so, you can keep track of the information you gather and the conclusions you reach. You can use your notebook to refer to experiments you have done, which may help you in doing future projects. Since you will be making many calculations, you will find it helpful to have a calculator nearby to analyze the data you collect.

Science Fairs

Most of the projects in this book may be appropriate for a science fair. Those projects are indicated with an asterisk (*). However, judges at such fairs do not reward projects or experiments that are simply copied from a book. For example, plugging numbers into a formula you do not understand will not impress judges. A graph of data collected from experiments you have done that is used to find a relationship between two variables would be more likely to receive serious consideration.

Science fair judges tend to reward creative thought and imagination. It is difficult to be creative or imaginative unless you are really interested in your project. Consequently, be sure to choose a subject that appeals to you. And before you jump into a project, consider, too, your own talents and the cost of materials you will need.

If you decide to use a project found in this book for a science fair, you should find ways to modify or extend it. This should not be difficult, because you will probably discover that as you do these projects, ideas for new experiments will come to mind—experiments that could make excellent science fair projects, particularly because the ideas are your own and are interesting to you.

If you decide to enter a science fair and have never done so before, you should read some of the books listed in the bibliography, as well as *Science Fair Projects—Planning, Presenting, Succeeding*, which is one of the books in this series. These books deal specifically with science fairs and will provide plenty of helpful hints and useful information that will enable you to avoid the pitfalls that sometimes plague first-time entrants. You will learn how to prepare appealing reports that include charts and graphs, how to set up and display your work, how to present your project, and how to relate to judges and visitors.

Safety First

The projects included in this book are perfectly safe. However, the following safety rules are well worth reading before you start any project.

1. Do any experiments or projects, whether from this book or of your own design, under the supervision of a science teacher or other knowledgeable adult.

2. Read all instructions carefully before proceeding with a project. If you have questions, check with your supervisor before going any further.

3. Maintain a serious attitude while conducting experiments. Fooling around can be dangerous to you and to others.

4. Wear approved safety goggles when you are working with a flame or doing anything that might cause injury to your eyes.

5. Do not eat or drink while experimenting.

6. Have a first-aid kit nearby while you are experimenting.

7. Do not put your fingers or any object other than properly designed electrical connectors into electrical outlets.

8. Never experiment with household electricity except under the supervision of a knowledgeable adult.

9. Do not touch a lit, high-wattage bulb. Lightbulbs produce light, but they also produce heat.

10. Many substances are poisonous. Do not taste them unless instructed to do so.

11. Keep flammable materials such as alcohol away from flames and other sources of heat.

12. If a thermometer breaks, inform your supervisor. Do not touch either the mercury or the broken glass with your bare hands.

1

Math and Science in Many Places

Mathematics is used to investigate many things. In later chapters you will have a chance to use mathematics as you do experiments related to light; temperature and heat; angles and heights; distance, time, and velocity; and sports. In this chapter you will explore great circles on the earth, properties of different varieties of apples, volume, mass, and density, as well as scaling, the golden ratio, and world population figures, all of which have a mathematical flavor.

1-1*
Great Circles: Measuring on a Sphere and Scaling

Find Chicago and Beijing on a globe. What are the approximate latitudes of these two cities? An airplane flying from Chicago to Beijing will not fly along a line

of latitude. Its flight path is usually across the Arctic. To see why airplanes follow such a route, you will need some string and a meterstick or yardstick and the globe. Calibrate the string by first putting it around the globe's equator. Place the length of string equal to the globe's equator on a meterstick or yardstick. What is the distance around the globe's equator in centimeters or inches? The actual distance around the earth's equator is 40,000 km (24,900 mi). Use this information and your measurement to find the globe's scale; that is, the distance on the globe represented by 1.0 cm or 1.0 in.

Determine the distance from Chicago to Beijing on the globe if the distance is measured along a line of latitude. Use the same string to find the shortest distance from Chicago to Beijing. Record that distance. Why do airplanes fly over the Arctic when traveling between these two cities?

Use the string and globe to find the shortest flight paths between various cities that are far apart. Cars, trucks, and even oceangoing ships often do not follow the shortest routes along the earth's surface. Why?

The shortest paths between cities that you measured on the globe lie along what are called great circles. A great circle is a circle on the surface of a sphere where the center of that circle lies at the center of the sphere. Such a circle divides the globe into two equal hemispheres. Are any lines of latitude great circles? Which lines of longitude are great circles?

10

1-2*
Testing Apples: Measuring, Averaging, Finding Volumes

Buy a few apples of different varieties at a supermarket. Use a measuring tape to find the circumference of, or distance around, each apple. If you do not have a measuring tape, use a string and a meterstick or yardstick as you did in the previous experiment to find the circumferences of the apples. What is the average circumference of each variety of apple? (The average circumference of one variety of apple would be the sum of the circumferences of all the apples of that variety divided by the number of apples in that variety.) Do the average circumferences of different varieties of apples differ?

Weigh all the apples of each variety on a balance. Record the weights. Do the average weights of different varieties of apples differ? If they do, which variety is the heaviest? Which variety is the lightest?

To find the volumes of these same apples, you will need a clear cylindrical container with a diameter greater than that of the largest apple. You can convert the container to a graduated cylinder by measuring out known volumes of water and pouring them into the container. A piece of masking tape down the side of the cylinder

Things you will need:

- adult supervisor
- several different varieties of apples (about 6 of each variety)
- measuring tape, or a string and a meterstick or yardstick
- pencil and paper
- balance or scale
- clear, cylindrical container (with a diameter greater than that of the largest apple)
- measuring cup and water
- masking tape
- marking pen
- long thin stick
- small aluminum pans (one for each variety of apple)
- knife
- oven
- pot holders
- popcorn

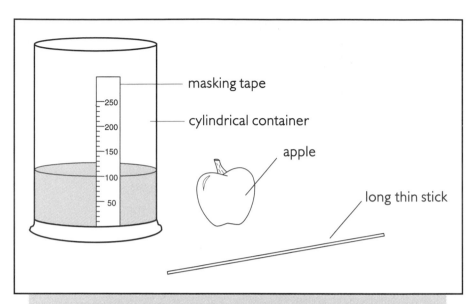

Figure 1. A clear, cylindrical container can be used to measure the volume of an apple. This container currently holds 100 ml of water. What will be the water level when the apple is submerged? How can you find the apple's volume?

will allow you to mark each volume of water added to the container with a line that has the proper number beside it (see Figure 1).

Empty the container. Pour a convenient volume of water into the cylinder and record the volume according to the marks you have made. Add an apple. Does the apple sink or float? What does this tell you about the apple's density?

If the apple floats, you can use a long thin stick to push the apple beneath the water. How much water does the apple displace? What is the apple's volume? Repeat this process for each apple. What is the average volume of each variety of apple? Do the average volumes of different apple varieties differ?

Taste each apple. Can you tell which kind of apple contains the largest percentage of water? Record the variety that you think holds the most water per gram of apple.

To test your prediction, you can measure the percentage of water in the apples by doing an experiment. Choose an apple from each of the varieties you bought. Next, gather as many small aluminum pans as you have apples. On a piece of masking tape, write a number and the name of the apple variety you plan to place in the pan. Put the tape on the aluminum and weigh the pan. After you weigh the pan, place an apple in it and reweigh. Record the number of each pan as well as its weight with the apple in it. How can you find the weight of the apple alone?

Under adult supervision, cut each apple into thin slices in the pan. Place all the pans in an oven at 120°F and heat the apples for several hours. If your oven does not have a setting for 120°F, set the oven to Warm. The heat will make the apples dry faster.

Use a pot holder to remove the pans from the oven. After the pans cool, reweigh each one. Repeat the process of heating and weighing until the apples show no further weight loss.

Calculate the weight loss of each apple. Since the change in the weight of each apple was due to loss of water, how much water did each apple lose? What percentage of each apple's original weight was water? Which variety of apple held the most water per gram of apple? (Be careful not to include the weight of the pan.) Was it the one you predicted? Which variety held the least amount of water per gram of apple?

Exploring on Your Own

Try a similar experiment with popcorn. Weigh the popcorn before and after popping. Does the popcorn lose weight during popping? If so, what percentage of its weight did it lose? Do you think the weight of the popped popcorn will change if you dry it in an oven as you did the apples? Try it! What percentage of popcorn, by weight, is water?

Which foods do you think contain very little water? Which foods do you think contain a high percentage of water? Test your predictions experimentally. What do you find?

1-3*
Volume, Mass, and Density

How is the volume of a substance related to its mass or weight? In this experiment you will be measuring mass. The mass of a substance can be found on a beam balance, which is a bar with a pan on either or both ends, or on a scale. Any object placed on a beam balance will give the same reading everywhere. On the other hand, a spring balance measures weight. An object suspended from a spring balance will weigh more on earth than on the moon because the moon's gravity is weaker. Because the moon does not pull as hard on an object as the earth, the spring will be stretched less on the moon than on the earth. A beam balance gives the same reading on the moon as it does on the earth because gravity has the same effect on the pan on one side of the balance as it does on the other.

Things you will need:
- beam balance or scale
- graduated cylinder or metric measuring cup
- standard masses
- cold water
- graph paper
- pencil
- ruler
- rubbing alcohol
- clay
- thread

To find out how the mass of a substance is related to its volume, place a graduated cylinder or metric measuring cup on a pan on one side of a balance. Place standard masses (weights) on the other pan until the beam is balanced. Record the vessel's mass in grams. Add 100 ml of cold water to the cylinder and record its mass again. How can you find the mass of the water alone? Record the mass and volume of the water. Repeat the experiment for volumes of 80, 60, 40, and 20 ml of water.

Use the data you have collected to plot a graph of mass, on the vertical axis, versus volume, on the horizontal axis, as shown in Figure 2. Use a ruler to draw the best straight line you can through the points you have plotted. What is the slope (rise ÷ run) for this

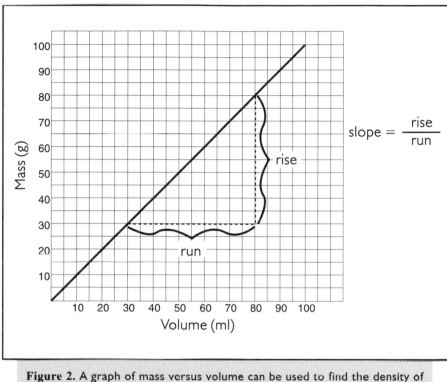

$$\text{slope} = \frac{\text{rise}}{\text{run}}$$

Figure 2. A graph of mass versus volume can be used to find the density of a substance.

graph? Make several different measurements of the slope. Do all your measurements of the slope agree? What are the units of the slope: grams (g), milliliters (ml), grams per milliliter (g/ml), or milliliters per gram (ml/g)?

As you discovered, the slope of the graph you made has units of g/ml because in finding the slope you divided mass, in grams, by volume, in milliliters. Furthermore, since the graph has the same slope everywhere, the ratio of mass to volume will be the same wherever you choose to measure the slope.

The slope of a graph of mass versus volume gives you the density of the substance on which the measurements were made. What is the density of water according to your graph?

A liter is equal to 1,000 milliliters (ml) or 1,000 cubic centimeters (cm^3). What is the density of water in grams per cubic centimeter (g/cm^3)? In grams per liter (g/l)?

Exploring on Your Own

You might guess that different substances have different densities. To see if you are right, repeat the experiment, using rubbing alcohol instead of water. What is the slope of this graph? What is the density of rubbing alcohol? Is it different from the density of water?

As you have found, the density of a substance is the ratio of its mass to its volume. Graphs of mass versus volume for all substances will resemble those you made for water and alcohol. The slopes of these graphs show that the ratio of mass to volume is always the same for any given substance regardless of the amount measured. The value of that ratio (the density of the substance) is given by the slope of the graph and is different for most substances.

To find the density of any object, all you have to do is measure its mass and volume and divide the mass by the volume. To find the density of a solid with a regular shape, such as a cube or other parallelepiped (a six-faced figure), a cylinder, a cone, or a sphere, you can measure its dimensions, calculate its volume, and then find its mass on a balance.

To find the density of an irregularly shaped object such as a lump of clay, first weigh the clay on a balance. Then, roll the clay around a thread into a shape that will fit into a graduated cylinder or measuring cup. (Does changing the shape of the clay affect its mass?) Partially fill the graduated cylinder or measuring cup with water and record the volume of water in it. Lower the clay into the water until it is completely submerged. How can you find the volume of the clay from the change in the water level? How can you find the density of the clay? What is the clay's density in grams per milliliter (g/ml)? What is the density of clay in grams per cubic centimeter (g/cm^3)?

1-4*
Scaling and Ratios

Things you will need:

- clay
- ruler
- two plastic containers with about the same volume, one shaped like a pancake and one a tall cylinder
- thermometer
- clock or watch with a second hand
- graduated cylinder or metric measuring cup
- hot tap water (50°C or 120°F or hotter)

Use clay to make a cube that is 1.0 cm on a side. Based on what you found about the density of clay in the previous experiment, what is the mass of the cube?

As a first approximation, assume the cube of clay represents an animal. What is the animal's total (a) surface area? (b) volume? (c) mass?

Use clay to make a cube that is twice as wide, tall, and long as the cube you made before. Again, let this cube represent an animal. What is this animal's total (a) surface area? (b) volume? (c) mass?

You have made two "animals." Compare them by finding the ratio of their (a) heights; (b) surface areas; (c) volumes; (d) masses.

As you have seen, the ratio of surface area to volume (or weight) is larger for a small body, such as a cube of clay 1.0 cm on a side, than for a large body, such as a cube of clay 2.0 cm on a side. The rate that heat is lost from a warm-blooded animal's body depends on its surface area. After all, it is the surface of the animal's body that is in contact with the cooler surroundings, be it air or water.

The relationship between the rate that heat is lost from a body and the body's surface area can be investigated experimentally. You will need two plastic containers, one shaped like a pancake (a flattened cylinder) and the other with a tall cylindrical shape. When these two containers holding equal volumes of water cool, they cool very differently. In addition to the two different cylinders, you will need a graduated cylinder or metric measuring cup, a thermometer, hot water, and a clock or watch with a second hand.

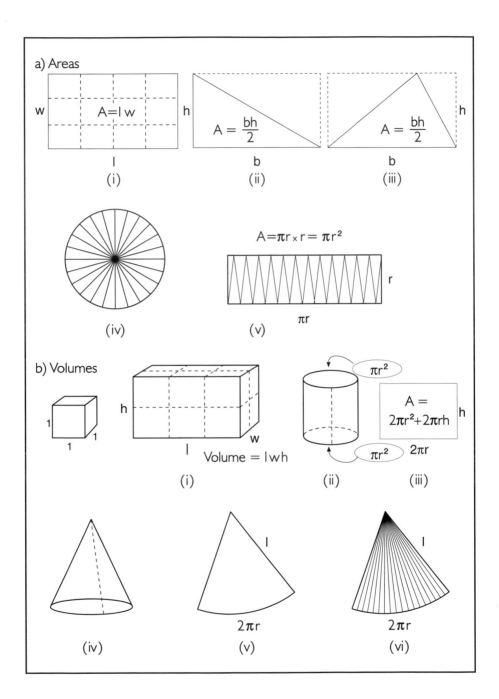

Figure 3. a) AREAS: Areas are measured in square units. A square 1.0 cm on a side has an area of 1.0 square centimeter (cm²). *i* The area of a rectangle l units long and w units wide has, as the drawing shows, an area of l x w. In the drawing, l is 4 units and w is 3 units. If the units are centimeters, the area is 12 cm². *ii* A right triangle is half a rectangle, so its area is 1/2 bh. Can you show that this same formula holds for the triangle in *iii* and, in fact, for all triangles? *iv* A circle can be "sliced" into a large number of triangles with altitudes equal to the circle's radius and bases at the circumference so small that the curvature is negligible. *v* When the triangles are put together in alternate fashion as shown, they form a rectangle with an altitude of r and a total base equal to half the circle's circumference or $\pi d/2 = \pi r$. The product of the rectangle's base and altitude gives the area of the circle: $\pi r \times r = \pi r^2$.

b) VOLUMES AND AREAS OF THREE-DIMENSIONAL OBJECTS: *i* The basic unit of volume is a cube 1 unit wide, long, and high. If the units are centimeters, then its volume is 1 cm x 1 cm x 1 cm = 1 cm³. The parallelepiped shown is 3 units long, 2 units wide, and 2 units high. As you can see, its volume contains 12 basic units, which equals l x w x h. Its volume, therefore, is equal to the area of the base (l x w) times the height. If the units are centimeters, then the volume is 3 cm x 2 cm x 2 cm = 12 cm³.

The volume of a cylinder (*ii*), like the volume of all regular solids, is equal to the area of the base x the height. Since the base of a cylinder is a circle, the volume of a cylinder is πr^2 x h. The surface area of a cylinder is the area of top and bottom, $2 \times \pi r^2$, + the area of its round sides, which is πdh. To see where the πdh comes from, notice that if the sides of the cylinder are opened along the dotted line shown in *ii* and then flattened, they form a rectangle, as shown in *iii*, whose base is the circumference of the circular top and bottom of the cylinder, a length of πd or $2\pi r$, and whose altitude is the height of the cylinder, h. Thus, the total area of a cylinder is $2\pi r^2 + \pi dh$ or $2\pi r^2 + 2\pi rh$.

A circular cone, *iv*, has a base with an area of πr^2. When opened along the dotted line shown in *iv* and flattened, the sides of the cone form a surface (*v*) that can be thought of as a series of very narrow triangles (*vi*) with altitudes equal to l, the slant height of the cone. The total length of the bases of all the little triangles is the circumference of the cone's base, $2\pi r$. Since the area of each little triangle is equal to 1/2 its base times its altitude, the surface area of the cone's sides is $1/2(2\pi rl)$. The total surface area of the cone is $\pi r^2 + \pi rl$.

Can you show that the volume of a cone is $1/3\ \pi r^2 h$? Can you show that the volume of a sphere is $4/3\ \pi r^3$ and that its total surface area is $4\pi r^2$?

Use the graduated cylinder or metric measuring cup to measure out 100 ml of tap water that is 50°C (120°F) or hotter. Pour the hot water into the pancake-shaped cylinder. When the water temperature reaches 40°C (105°F), measure how long it takes the water to cool to 35°C (95°F). Repeat the experiment, using the same volume of hot water in the tall cylinder.

How much time was required for the water temperature in the pancake-shaped container to fall 5°C (or 10°F)? How much time was required for the water temperature in the tall container to fall 5°C (or 10°F)? Heat loss in this case can be measured by the decrease in temperature. The rate at which heat is lost can be found by dividing the change in temperature by the time required for the temperature change to occur. In which container did the water lose heat faster? What is the rate of heat loss, in degrees per minute, for the water in each container?

To compare the surface area of the water in the two containers, pour 100 ml of water into both containers. Measure the diameter of each container and the depth of the water in it. Use your measurements to calculate the surface areas of the two samples of hot water in square centimeters (cm^2). (Figure 3 provides some useful information about surface areas and volumes for a number of different shapes. This information will be useful in other experiments as well.)

How did the ratio of the rate of heat flow from the two samples of hot water compare with the ratio of their surface areas? If they are nearly the same, then

$$\frac{\text{Surface area of pancake cylinder}}{\text{Surface area of tall cylinder}} = \frac{\text{rate of heat loss from pancake cylinder}}{\text{rate of heat loss from regular cylinder}}$$

If this is the case, then you can conclude that the rate of heat loss is proportional to the surface area through which the heat flows. Of course, there are experimental errors and other factors such as differences in the thickness of the containers, so the ratios may not be identical. Experimental errors involve the unavoidable limits of accuracy in making measurements of length, mass, time, and volume. With better instruments, experimental errors would be reduced.

How can you use your measurements of diameter and water depth for the two cylinders to confirm the fact that both cylinders contained 100 ml, or 100 cm^3, of water?

1-5*
The Golden Ratio

Pythagoras was a Greek philosopher who believed that all beauty and knowledge was to be found in numbers and their relationships. Musicians will tell you that the ratio of the frequencies of two notes, a topic first investigated by Pythagoras, determines whether or not they are harmonious. Early architects claimed that the key to beauty in architecture is the golden ratio.

Things you will need:

• paper

• ruler

• protractor

• pencil

• drawing compass

• picture of Parthenon

• buildings and pictures of buildings

• measuring tape

• a number of different people

The golden ratio, so named because objects with dimensions in this ratio were believed to have great beauty, was discovered through a geometric construction. You can discover the golden ratio for yourself by using a ruler, a protractor, and a sharp pencil to draw a square 10 cm on a side like the one shown in the scaled drawing in Figure 4a. Extend the base line *WX* to a point near the edge of the paper. Divide the square you have drawn into two equal rectangles, *UMNW* and *MVXN*, as shown by the dotted line. Then use a drawing compass to draw the arc of a circle with a radius equal to the diagonal of the rectangle *MVXN* as shown in 4b. The arc should meet the extended base of the original square you drew. Next, construct a rectangle *VXYZ* as shown in Figure 4c, whose base is the extended base of the square that intercepts the arc. Use the original height of the square as the height of the new rectangle.

The ratio of the height of the rectangle you just drew to its base ($VX \div XY$) is defined as the golden ratio, and the rectangle *VXYZ* is a golden rectangle. According to your measurements, what is the golden ratio? How closely does your value agree with the actual value, which is very close to 1.618, or about 8/5?

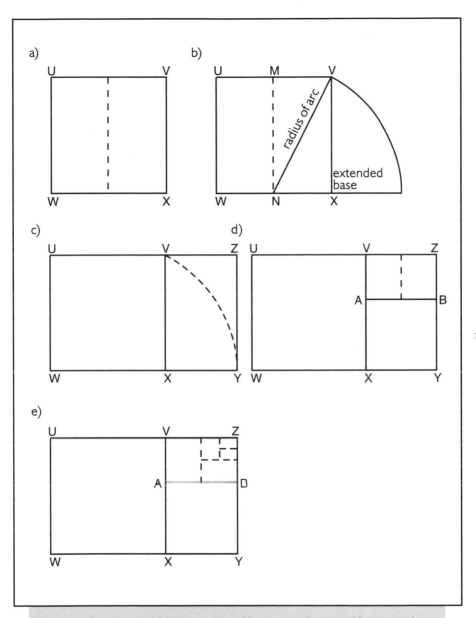

Figure 4. Constructions leading to the golden ratio and many golden rectangles.

There are a number of reasons why Greek mathematicians and architects regarded the golden ratio with such reverence. The ratio of the length of the original square and its extended base, $WX + XY$, to the original base, WX, is the golden ratio. Furthermore, if you construct a square within a golden rectangle—$ABYX$ in Figure 4d— the rectangle that remains, $ABZV$, is a golden rectangle. And a square constructed in that rectangle will leave a new, smaller golden rectangle. The process can go on indefinitely, giving rise to smaller and smaller golden rectangles (Figure 4e).

Notice, too, if $WX = 1.618$ and $XY = 1$, then

$$(1.618 + 1) \div 1.618 = 1.618.$$

Also, look at a series of numbers where each number is the sum of the two preceding ones, as, for example:

$$1, 1, 2, 3, 5, 8, 13, 21, 34, 55 \ldots.$$

The golden ratio forms a series of numbers such that when raised to increasing powers, each term is the sum of the two preceding terms.

$$(1.618)^0, (1.618)^1, (1.618)^2, (1.618)^3, (1.618)^4, (1.618)^5 \ldots.$$

Try it using the y^x key on a calculator. For example, to obtain 1.618^3, enter 1.618, press the y^x key, and then press 3, followed by the equal sign. You should find it produces a series that looks like this:

$$1, 1.618, 2.618, 4.236, 6.854, 11.09 \ldots.$$

Can you find any other number that works?
How about 1?

$$1^0, 1^1, 1^2, 1^3, 1^4, 1^5 \ldots.$$

Clearly, 1 does not work because 1 raised to any power is 1. (Remember, any number raised to the 0 power is 1.)

24

Does the number 2 work? How about 3? Can you find any number other than the golden ratio that works?

If you have seen the Parthenon, built in Athens in the fifth century B.C., or pictures of it, you will find that it was built with the golden ratio in mind. Make some measurements of pictures of the Parthenon and other buildings or of buildings themselves. Can you find the golden ratio in the structure of any of these buildings? Do you find buildings with the golden ratio to be more attractive than square buildings or buildings with rectangles other than the golden rectangle?

Le Corbusier, a twentieth-century architect, whose real name was Charles-Édouard Jeanneret (1887–1965), found the golden ratio in the structure of the human body. You can look for the ratio yourself. Begin by using a measuring tape to find the following lengths in a number of different people. Be sure to use the same units (centimeters or inches) in all your measurements. Measurements that require subtracting one value from another are indicated by the minus sign (–).

Height

Distance from floor to navel

Distance from navel to top of head

Distance from floor to tip of fingers of arm raised straight upward

Length of upper arm

Distance from tip of nose to tip of fingers when arm is fully outstretched to side

Distance between tips of left-hand and right-hand fingers when both arms are outstretched

Span (distance between tips of thumb and index finger of one outstretched hand)

Distance from top of head to tip of fingers of arm raised straight upward

Inseam (length of inside of leg)

Cubit (elbow to tip of middle finger)

Length of lower leg (knee to heel)

Height – Inseam

Height – Distance from floor to navel

Distance from floor to tip of fingers of arm raised straight upward – Distance from floor to navel

Distance from floor to navel – Inseam

Look at the measurements you have made. Which ones can be paired to form ratios equal to, or very nearly equal to (± 0.2), the golden ratio. If the ratio of a pair of measurements is equal to the golden ratio for one person, is it equal or nearly equal for other people as well?

1-6*
World Population

Table 1 contains estimates of the world's population since 1650. Plot a graph of world population on the vertical axis versus time on the horizontal axis. Allow space to extrapolate (extend) the graph to 2050. According to the graph you have made, during what years has the world's population grown the fastest?

Things you will need:
- graph paper
- pencil
- ruler
- access to public library

To check the analysis you made from the graph, divide the population growth (the change in population from one date to the next) by the number of years during which the growth occurred. Do the numbers you obtain by these divisions agree with the analysis you made from the graph?

Extrapolate your graph, as best you can, to the year 2010. How confident are you about extrapolating the graph to 2050? What do you estimate the population will be in 2010? Assuming your estimate of the world's population in 2010 is accurate, by what average percentage is the world's population increasing each year? How long will it take for the world's population to double at that percentage rate of increase?

Table 1: World population figures from 1650 to 1995

Year	Population (in billions)	Year	Population (in billions)
1650	0.550	1900	1.600
1750	0.725	1950	2.556
1850	1.175	1980	4.458
		1995	5.734

One way to estimate the doubling time makes use of the rule of 72. According to this rule, if you divide 72 by the annual percentage increase, you will obtain the number of years for the quantity to double. For example, if the annual population increase is 10 percent, the population will double in 7.2 years (72 ÷ 10). Another approach is to use the y^x key on a calculator. If the population increase is 10 percent per year, then the population after one year will be 1.10 times greater than it was the previous year. Enter 1.1, press the y^x key, then press the number representing your guess for the years required for the population to double, followed by the equal sign. If the answer is about 2.0, your guess was right. If not, try again until you get an answer of approximately 2.0.

In 1995 the population of the United States was 263.8 million. What percentage of the world's people lived in the United States? In the same year the birth rate in the United States was 15.1 live births per 1,000 people; the death rate was 8.7 deaths per 1,000 people. At what rate was the United States population increasing per 1,000 people? At what rate was it increasing in terms of percentage? At this rate, how long will it take for our population to double?

Determine the earth's total land area. You can do this by first calculating the earth's total area and then taking into account the fact that 70 percent of the earth is covered by water. Remember the area of a sphere is $4\pi r^2$ and the earth's diameter is 12,700 km (7,900 mi). How much land, in square meters, is there per person if today's population is 6 billion people? How much land is there per person in square feet?

An acre of land is 43,560 square feet. How many acres of land per person are available to today's population of 6 billion?

Exploring on Your Own

Some people believe that the world's population will grow to about 12 billion during the next century. If that happens, how much land, in square meters, will be available per person? How many square feet per person? How many acres per person?

Do some research to find out how much of the world's land can be used to grow crops and animals for food. How many people can be fed if all the land is used to produce food? What is the maximum population that the earth can support?

2

Math and Light

In this chapter you will investigate the angles made by light when it is reflected from mirrors and other smooth surfaces, the strange behavior of light when it passes from air to water, how the sizes of shadows change with distance, and the images formed when light passes through pinholes. In all of these investigations, you will see the vital role that mathematics plays in helping us understand the behavior of light.

2-1*
Angles and Reflected Light

We see light as something diffuse, something that fills space with a bright but weightless "substance." If we look at a narrow beam of light, we can observe its nature more clearly.

To make such a beam, use scissors to cut a vertical slit about 1 mm (1/16 in) wide in the middle of two 10 cm x 15 cm (4 in x 6 in) index cards. Fold the ends of the cards so that they will stand upright. Place them on a white sheet of paper about

Things you will need:

• scissors

• two 10 cm x 15 cm (4 in x 6 in) index cards

• white sheet of paper

• 100-watt or stronger lightbulb and socket

• plane mirror

• clay

• pencil

• ruler

• protractor

1 m (3 ft) in front of a bright lightbulb in an otherwise dark room, as shown in Figure 5a. Adjust the height of the lightbulb so that the light coming through the two slits produces a long narrow beam on the paper. The light coming through the first slit (the one closest to the lightbulb) will widen slightly. The second slit will eliminate the widening and provide a narrow beam with sides that are nearly parallel.

The narrow beam you have made can be thought of as a light ray. In theory, a ray of light represents the direction that light is traveling, and, like any line, has no width. However, the narrow beam you have made is easily seen and makes a reasonable substitute for a theoretical ray.

Place a plane (flat) mirror upright to the light ray, as shown in Figure 5b. As you can see, the ray bounces (reflects) off the mirror. What happens when you slowly turn the upright mirror as shown by the wide arrows? How does the angle between the mirror and the reflected ray of light (angle b) change as you make the angle

31

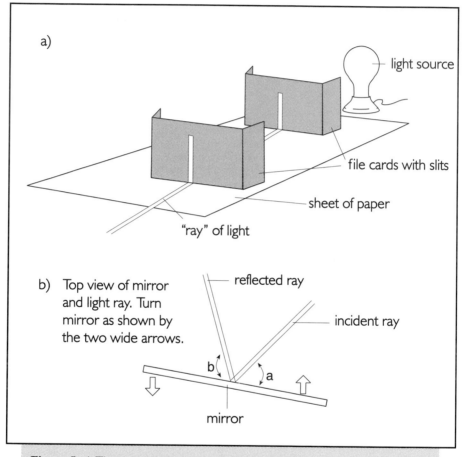

a)

light source

file cards with slits

sheet of paper

"ray" of light

b) Top view of mirror and light ray. Turn mirror as shown by the two wide arrows.

reflected ray

incident ray

b

a

mirror

Figure 5. a) The two slits produce a "ray" of light. b) A mirror reflects the ray. How do angles *a* and *b* compare?

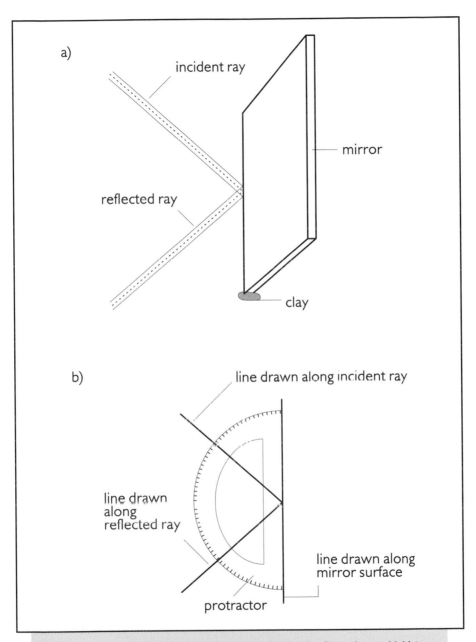

Figure 6. a) Make dotted lines along the incident and reflected rays. b) Using a protractor, measure angles *a* and *b*. How do they compare?

between the incident ray (the ray from the lightbulb) and the mirror (angle *a*) smaller? As you make angle *a* larger?

Use a small lump of clay to support the mirror upright on a sheet of paper. Draw a line on the paper along the mirror's rear surface. With the mirror's rear surface on the line, let the incident light ray strike the mirror at an angle. Use a pencil to make dotted lines along the incident and reflected rays, as shown in Figure 6a. Remove the mirror and use a ruler to connect the dotted lines that represent the incident and reflected rays. Use the same ruler to extend the line that marked the mirror's rear surface. With a protractor, measure the angle between the mirror and the incident ray that you drew, as shown in Figure 6b. Measure, too, the angle between the reflected ray and the mirror. How do the two angles compare?

Repeat the experiment a number of times, being careful to obtain a wide range of different angles between the mirror and the incident ray. For each case, how does the angle between the incident ray and the mirror compare with the angle between the

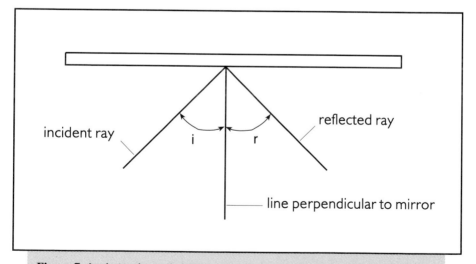

Figure 7. Angle *i* is the angle between the incident ray and a perpendicular to the mirror. Angle *r* is the angle between the reflected ray and the same perpendicular.

reflected ray and the mirror? What conclusion can you draw about these two angles?

Physicists define the angle between the incident ray and a line perpendicular to the mirror where the incident ray strikes the mirror as the angle of incidence ($\angle i$; see Figure 7). The angle between the same perpendicular and the reflected ray is defined as the angle of reflection ($\angle r$). How can you find $\angle i$ and $\angle r$ as defined by physicists for the angles you measured in each of the experiments you did without making any additional measurements? What can you conclude about $\angle i$ and $\angle r$? What rule or law of nature seems to hold true for these two angles regardless of their size? What is the largest possible angle of incidence? What is the largest possible angle of reflection?

At what angle of incidence do the incident and reflected rays lie along the same line? Does the rule you made still hold true under this condition?

2-2*

Mirrors in Glass and Water: Measuring More Angles

Things you will need:

• pencil

• ruler

• white paper

• sheet of corrugated cardboard

• plane mirror

• clay

• 4 pins

• protractor

• plastic box about 10 cm (4 in) x 5 cm (2 in) x 8 cm (3 in) deep

• water

• 2 index cards with slits from previous experiment

• 100-watt or stronger lightbulb and socket

Using a pencil and a ruler, draw a straight line near one end of a sheet of white paper, and lay the paper on corrugated cardboard. Place a plane mirror so that its rear edge is on the line you drew. A lump of clay can be used to support the mirror, as shown in Figure 8a. Place two pins in a line at an angle to the mirror as shown. The two pins, P_1 and P_2, establish a line (an incident ray of light) leading to the mirror.

Now go to the other side of the paper and use two more pins, P_3 and P_4, to find the reflected ray of light. You can do this by using your eye to line up pins P_3 and P_4 with the mirror images of pins P_1 and P_2. When you have finished, pins P_3 and P_4 and the images of pins P_1 and P_2 should all appear to lie in a straight line, as shown in Figure 8b.

Remove the mirror and use a ruler and pencil to draw straight lines connecting pins P_1 and P_2 and pins P_3 and P_4 to the line that marked the plane of the mirror. These two lines represent the incident and reflected rays. You can confirm this by using a protractor to measure the angles that existed between the rays and the mirror. Are the two angles equal?

Repeat the experiment, but this time place the mirror in a plastic box filled with water, as shown in Figure 9. The mirror should

36

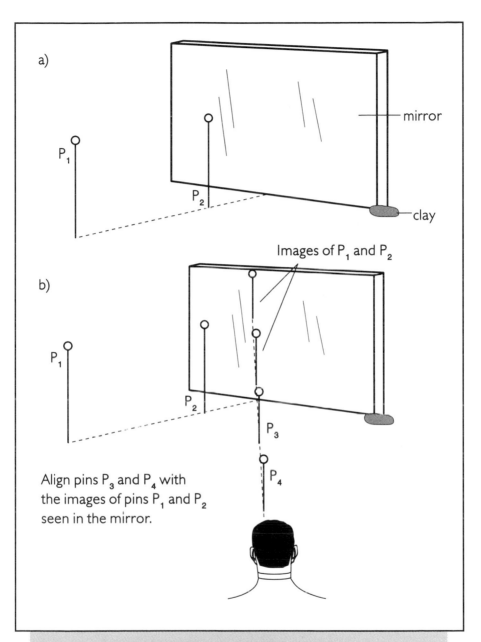

a)

P_1

mirror

P_2

clay

Images of P_1 and P_2

b)

P_1

P_2

P_3

Align pins P_3 and P_4 with
the images of pins P_1 and P_2
seen in the mirror.

P_4

Figure 8. a) Pins P_1 and P_2 define a ray of light (the incident ray) that strikes the mirror. b) Pins P_3 and P_4, when aligned with the images of pins P_1 and P_2, define the reflected ray.

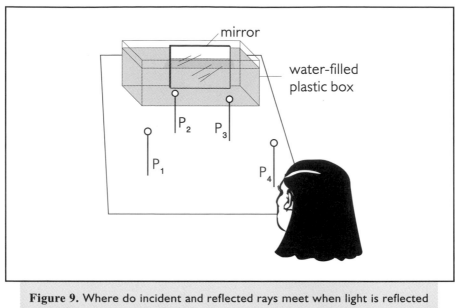

Figure 9. Where do incident and reflected rays meet when light is reflected in water?

be against the far side of the box, with its rear surface on the line on the paper. Light from pins P_1 and P_2 must now pass through the water before being reflected. Again, use your eye to line up pins P_3 and P_4 with the mirror images of pins P_1 and P_2. When you have finished, pins P_3 and P_4 and the images of pins P_1 and P_2 should all appear to lie on a straight line.

Use a ruler and pencil to draw straight lines along the incident ray (established by pins P_1 and P_2) and the reflected ray (pins P_3 and P_4). Where do these two rays meet this time? Can you explain why they meet there? Is there anything to reflect light at the point where they meet?

Exploring on Your Own

To see why the rays appear to meet where they do, set up the box of water and the mirror as before. This time, use the lightbulb and cards with slits in them that you used in the previous experiment to

38

form a ray of light. Let this light ray reflect off the mirror after passing through the water. What happens to the ray of light as it passes from air into water? What happens to the ray when it strikes the mirror? What happens to the ray as it passes from water back into air?

Now see if you can explain the intersection of the two rays established by the four pins.

2-3*
Shadow Size: Scaled Drawings and Ratios

Place a lamp with a clear light-bulb that has a straight horizontal filament several meters from a white or light-colored wall, as shown in Figure 10. Turn the bulb so that the filament is perpendicular to the wall. The filament, when viewed from the wall, will look like a point of light. You can tell when the light is acting as if it were coming from a point by moving your hand between the lightbulb and the wall. The shadow of your hand should cast a single, very sharp shadow.

Things you will need:

- clear lightbulb with straight horizontal filament, 60-watt or stronger
- dark room
- white or light-colored wall
- meterstick or yardstick
- scissors
- ruler
- heavy black paper or cardboard
- clothespin
- a friend
- paper
- pencil

Move the bulb so that the end of the filament, which serves as a point of light, is exactly 2 m (or 2 yd) from the wall. Use scissors to cut a square 5.0 cm (or 2 in) on a side from heavy black paper or cardboard. Then use a clothespin to hold the square halfway between the point light source and the wall (1.0 m [or 1 yd] from the wall). Have a friend measure the shadow of the square on the wall. How wide is the shadow? How tall is the shadow? What is the area of the shadow? How does the size and appearance of the shadow support the idea that light travels in straight lines? If light did not travel in straight lines, what might the shadow look like?

Use a ruler to make a scale drawing (10 cm = 1.0 m) showing light rays coming from the point of light. In your two-dimensional drawing, you can represent the edge of the square with a line. How long should the line be on your drawing? How far should it be from the point of light on your drawing? How far should the wall be from the point of light on your drawing?

40

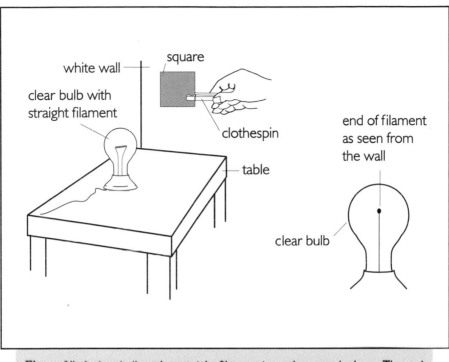

Figure 10. A clear bulb with a straight filament is used to cast shadows. The end of the filament can be used as a point source of light.

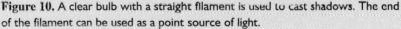

Draw a few of the light rays coming from the point of light that are blocked by the square. Then draw the rays that just pass over the top and bottom of the square. Use your scale drawing to determine how far apart those same rays are when they reach the wall. What represents the side view of the shadow in your drawing?

You can make another scale drawing and use it to predict the size of the shadow on the wall. In this drawing, place the square 0.5 m (or 18 in) from the point of light (1.5 m [or 1.5 yd] from the wall). According to your scale drawing, how large will the shadow on the wall be? What will its area be? Test your prediction by actually holding the square 1.5 m from the wall and having your friend measure the shadow. Is the shadow the size you predicted from your drawing?

From your drawings, try to develop a mathematical rule or formula that will allow you to predict the length and area of the shadow of the square when it is any distance from the wall and the point of light is 2 m (or 2 yd) from the wall. How wide is the shadow when the square is 25 cm from the wall? When the square is 50 cm from the wall? When it is 75 cm from the wall? How tall is the shadow when the square is 125 cm from the wall? When it is 175 cm from the wall?

Why can't the shadow ever be smaller than the square?

What does halving the distance between the square and the point of light do to the length of the shadow? What does it do to the area of the shadow? What does reducing the distance between the square and point of light to one quarter do to the length of the shadow? To the area of the shadow?

2-4*
Pinholes, Images, and Distances: Ratios, Formulas, and Graphs

Place a clear lightbulb in a socket on the floor of a room that can be darkened. Plug in the socket so that the bulb is lighted and the glowing filament can be seen. Measure the approximate distance from the floor to the bulb's filament. Place a large cardboard box that has had its top removed on one side of the light, as shown in Figure 11. The open side of the box should face the light. Use a large pin to make a hole in the bottom of the box, which has been turned to an upright position, as shown. The hole should be as far above the floor as the bulb's filament. Tape white paper to a sheet of cardboard. Stand the cardboard on the other side of the pinhole. The white paper will serve as a

Things you will need:

- clear lightbulb, 60-watt or stronger
- dark room
- socket and cord, or short lamp
- meterstick or yardstick
- electrical outlet
- large cardboard box, top removed
- large pin
- sheet of cardboard
- tape
- white paper
- pencil
- ruler
- pen with dark ink
- graph paper
- white index card

screen. If the cardboard is creased and bent, it will stand upright, and you will not have to hold it.

Darken the room, leaving only the clear lightbulb burning. You should be able to see an image of the bulb's filament on the screen. What happens to the size of the image as you move the screen farther from the pinhole? What happens to the size of the image as you move the screen closer to the pinhole? Can you explain why the image size changes as you do this?

43

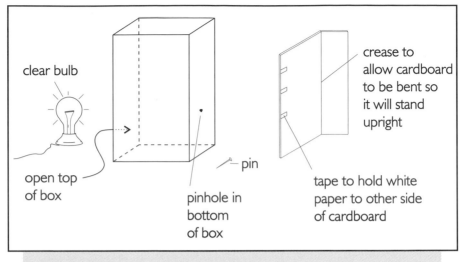

Figure 11. A box with a pinhole is placed between a clear lightbulb and a white screen. Can you see the image of the bulb's filament on the screen?

The image labels read:

clear bulb

open top of box

pinhole in bottom of box

pin

crease to allow cardboard to be bent so it will stand upright

tape to hold white paper to other side of cardboard

Is the image right-side up or upside down? Is it turned right for left? Even if you have a straight filament, you can still determine whether the image is upside down or turned right for left. Simply move a pencil slowly up and down in front of the bulb. The pencil's shadow will move across the image. How can you tell whether or not the image is upside down? How can you tell whether or not the image is turned right for left?

Figure 12a should help you understand how the image is formed. What assumption does the drawing make about light rays? Does the drawing also help you explain why the image's size changes as it moves closer to or farther from the pinhole?

To find out how the size of the image changes with distance, make a small scale on the screen, using a ruler and a dark pen, as shown in Figure 12b. The scale will allow you to measure the size of the image, either height or width, without having to place a ruler on the screen. Place the bulb's filament exactly 30 cm (1 ft) from the pinhole. Put the screen on the opposite side, at the same distance from the pinhole. How large is the image you see on the screen?

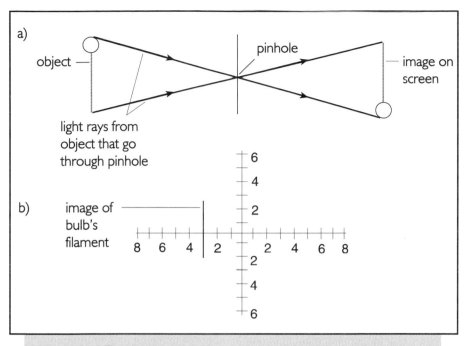

Figure 12. a) The diagram shows how an image is formed when light rays pass through a pinhole. b) A scale drawn on the white screen will help you determine the size of the image.

Now move the screen so that it is 60 cm (2 ft) from the pinhole. How large is the image now? How large is the image when the screen is 90 cm (3 ft) from the pinhole? When it is 120 cm (4 ft) from the pinhole?

Move the screen back toward the pinhole and check your measurements of image size for 120 cm, 90 cm, 60 cm, and 30 cm. Move the screen until it is only 15 cm (6 in) from the pinhole. How large is the image now? How large is it when it is 7.5 cm (3 in) from the pinhole?

With a pencil and graph paper, prepare a graph of image size versus the distance of the image from the pinhole. The axes for your graph are shown in Figure 13a. Draw the best straight line you can through the points you have made on the graph paper. Using the

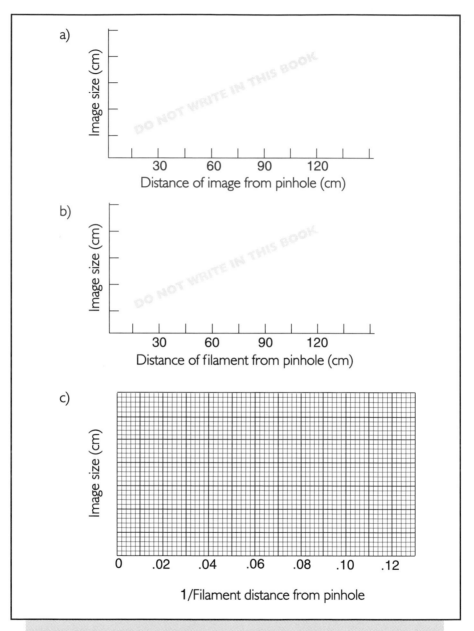

Figure 13. Axes for graphs relating size of pinhole images to a) distance of image from pinhole; b) distance of filament (or object) from pinhole; c) inverse of distance (1/distance) of filament from pinhole.

graph, predict the size of the image when the screen is 45 cm (18 in), 75 cm (30 in), and 105 cm (42 in) from the pinhole. Place the screen at these positions and measure the images. How closely do your measurements agree with your predictions?

Based on the drawing in Figure 12a and your own observations, at what distance from the pinhole do you think the image of the filament will be the same size as the filament itself? To find out if you are right, turn off the bulb. Wait for the bulb to cool off, then measure its filament as best you can through the glass. You might use what you learned about shadows in the previous experiment to determine the size of the filament. Now find the distance from the pinhole at which the image of the filament has the same length as the filament itself. Is it reasonably close to the size you predicted?

Exploring on Your Own

Try to formulate a rule or write an equation that allows you to predict the size of the image when the screen is at any distance from the pinhole.

What do you think will happen to the size of the image on the screen if you move the lightbulb closer to the pinhole? Try it. Were you right?

What do you think will happen to the size of the image if you move the lightbulb farther from the pinhole? Were you right?

To find out how the size of the image changes with the distance of the lightbulb's filament from the pinhole, begin with the bulb's filament exactly 30 cm (1 ft) from the pinhole. Put the screen on the other side of the pinhole at 60 cm (2 ft) from the pinhole and keep it at that position. How large is the image on the screen? Now move the filament so that it is 60 cm (2 ft) from the pinhole. How large is the image now? How large is the image when the filament is 90 cm (3 ft) from the pinhole? When it is 120 cm (4 ft) from the pinhole?

Move the bulb back toward the pinhole and check your measurements of image size when the filament is 120 cm, 90 cm,

60 cm, and 30 cm from the pinhole. Next, move the screen until it is only 15 cm (6 in) from the pinhole. How large is the image now? How large is it when the filament is 7.5 cm (3 in) from the pinhole?

With a pencil and graph paper, prepare a graph of image size versus the distance of the filament from the pinhole. The axes for your graph are shown in Figure 13b. Can you draw a straight line through the points you have made on the graph paper, or is the graph a curved line?

Try plotting your data on a graph with the axes shown in Figure 13c. In this graph, the image size is plotted against the inverse of the filament's distance from the pinhole. For example, when the filament is 15 cm from the pinhole, the inverse of that distance is 1/15, or 0.067. The data table in which you record the image size and inverse of distances would look like the one below.

Use the graph you have made to predict the size of the image when the filament is 45 cm (18 in), 75 cm (30 in), and 105 cm (42 in) from the pinhole. Place the filament at these positions and measure the images. How closely do the measurements agree with your predictions?

Try to formulate a rule or write an equation that allows you to predict the size of the image when the bulb's filament is at any

Distance of filament from pinhole, cm	Inverse of distance from pinhole (1/distance), cm	Size of image, cm
30	0.033	
60	0.017	
90	0.011	
120	0.0083	
15	0.067	
7.5	0.13	

distance from the pinhole. Now try to formulate a rule or write an equation that allows you to predict the size of the image when both the lightbulb's filament and the screen are at any distance from the pinhole.

Pinhole Images in Nature

On a bright, sunny, summer day, look at the ground in the shade of a large tree. You will see a number of circles of light amid the shade. They are called sun dapples. What might cause these circles of light? What does the circular shape suggest might be the source of the light that causes these sun dapples?

Could the sun shining through small openings between the leaves produce pinhole images of the sun? **Do not look directly at the sun! It can damage your eyes!** To see if images of the sun can be produced by pinholes, make a pinhole in a sheet of cardboard. Then hold the cardboard between the sun and a white index card that can serve as a screen. Can you find a pinhole image of the sun? What happens if you make two or three more pinholes near the first one you made in the cardboard? Do you now have several images of the sun?

Go back to the sun dapples you found in the shade. Measure a few of them. Are they all the same size? If not, can you explain why they differ in size?

The sun, which has a diameter of about 700,000 km (435,000 mi), is about 150 million km (93 million miles) from the earth. Using the sun's diameter and its distance from the earth, together with the size of any one circle of light beneath the tree, find the distance between the circle of light and the tiny opening between the leaves that produces the image.

3

Math, Temperature, and Heat

This chapter focuses on the mathematics related to measuring temperature and heat. You will investigate four different temperature scales. You are probably familiar with the Celsius and Fahrenheit scales, but the Kelvin and Rankine scales may be new to you. You will discover how mathematics is used to measure heat, how it enables us to find the heat needed to melt a gram of water (heat of fusion), boil away a gram of water (heat of vaporization), or determine the heat required to raise the temperature of one gram of any substance by one degree (specific heat).

3-1*
Temperature Scales: Graphs, Conversions

Celsius and Fahrenheit Scales

Things you will need:
- graph paper
- pencil
- ruler

In most countries weather reports give temperatures in degrees Celsius (°C). In the United States, temperatures are more often reported in degrees Fahrenheit (°F). How are these two scales related?

Both the Celsius and the Fahrenheit temperature scales are based on two fixed points—two temperatures that are determined by nature regardless of the scale used to measure them. These two fixed points are the temperature at which water freezes (or melts) and the temperature at which it boils (or condenses) when at atmospheric pressure, the pressure of the air at sea level (a barometer reading of 760 mm or 30 in of mercury).

On the Celsius scale, the freezing point of water is defined as 0°C; on the Fahrenheit scale, the same temperature is defined as 32°F. The temperature of boiling water on the Celsius scale is 100°C; on the Fahrenheit scale, it is 212°F.

Using these two fixed points, you can plot a graph like the one in Figure 14. It shows the temperature in degrees Fahrenheit along the vertical axis plotted against the corresponding temperatures in degrees Celsius along the horizontal axis. The two fixed points are indicated. On your graph you can use the fixed points to draw a straight line that extends to at least -50°F on the lower end and to 300°F on the upper end.

Use your graph to find the temperature in degrees Fahrenheit when the temperature in degrees Celsius is (a) 0°C; (b) 20°C; (c) 45°C; (d) 120°C; (e) -10°C; (f) -40°C. Then use the same graph to find the temperature in degrees Celsius when the Fahrenheit temperature is (a) 212°F; (b) 40°F; (c) 100°F; (d) 290°F; (e) 0°F; (f) -40°F.

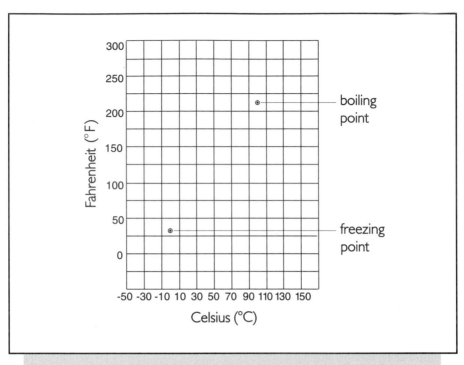

Figure 14. The freezing and boiling points of water serve as fixed temperatures on both the Celsius and Fahrenheit scales.

At what temperature do the two scales have the same numeric value?

You can write a formula that allows you to convert temperatures from one scale to the other. To begin, figure out the number of degrees between the freezing point and boiling point on each scale. How many degrees are there between these two fixed temperatures on the Fahrenheit scale? On the Celsius scale? How many degrees Fahrenheit are equal to one degree Celsius? How many degrees Celsius are equal to one degree Fahrenheit?

If the temperature on the Celsius scale is ten degrees above the freezing point, how many degrees is it above the freezing point on the Fahrenheit scale? Since the Fahrenheit scale begins not at 0° but at 32°, what number must be added to the number of Fahrenheit degrees above the freezing point to find the actual temperature in degrees Fahrenheit that corresponds to 10°C?

From what you have done, fill in the blanks in the equation below. This equation will allow you to convert temperatures from °C to °F.

$$°F = \underline{\quad} °C + \underline{\quad}$$

Does the equation work for negative temperatures?

See if you can similarly find an equation that will allow you to convert Fahrenheit temperatures to Celsius temperatures.

Celsius and Kelvin Scales

During the mid-nineteenth century, William Thomson, who became Lord Kelvin later in life, introduced another temperature scale. Thomson discovered that the coldest possible temperature, the temperature at which molecules would stop moving, was -273°C. He called this temperature absolute zero, because lower temperatures were impossible. To avoid negative temperatures, he invented what he called the absolute temperature scale. Today that scale is known as the Kelvin scale in honor of Lord Kelvin.

On the Kelvin scale, degrees are referred to as kelvins, and -273°C is defined as 0 K, not 0°K. The value of a kelvin is the same as a degree on the Celsius scale; that is, the temperature range between the freezing and boiling points of water is 100 kelvins. Because 0 K is equal to -273°C and a kelvin has the same value as a degree Celsius, the freezing point of water is 273 K on the Kelvin scale. What is the boiling point of water on the Kelvin scale?

Plot a graph of temperature in degrees Celsius on the vertical scale versus Kelvin temperatures on the horizontal axis. What is the temperature in degrees Celsius when the Kelvin temperature is (a) 0 K? (b) 273 K? (c) 373 K? (d) 323 K? (e) 423 K? (f) 100 K? What is the temperature in kelvins when the Celsius temperature is (a) 0°C? (b) -273°C? (c) 100°C? (d) 50°C? (e) 150°C? (f) -50°C?

Write an equation that allows you to convert any temperature on the Kelvin scale to degrees Celsius. Write another equation that allows you to convert temperatures on the Celsius scale to kelvins.

Rankine and Fahrenheit Scales

William Rankine invented yet another temperature scale. His scale made use of Kelvin's absolute zero but used degrees equal in value to the degrees on the Fahrenheit scale. On the Rankine scale, the value of a degree Rankine is the same as a degree Fahrenheit, but 0°R is absolute zero.

Exploring on Your Own

Using what you have learned, write equations that allow you to convert (a) Fahrenheit to Rankine; (b) Rankine to Fahrenheit; (c) Rankine to kelvins; (d) Rankine to Celsius.

3-2*
Measuring the Heat Delivered by a Heater

Because this experiment requires the use of household electricity, it should be done under adult supervision.

Heat is defined as the energy transferred between two substances because of a difference in their temperatures. Heat always "flows" from a warmer substance to a cooler one.

Early scientists believed that heat was an invisible, weightless fluid that flowed from warm bodies to cooler ones. That concept of heat persists today: We still speak of heat flowing from hot objects to cooler ones

even though we know the transfer is accomplished by collisions between molecules.

Heat is measured in units called calories or joules. A calorie (cal) is the heat transferred when the temperature of one gram of water rises by one degree Celsius. A joule is the heat transferred when one gram of water rises by 0.24°C. For your work, the calorie is the easier unit to use.

In this experiment, you will measure the heat delivered per minute by an immersion heater. Because you will be using an electrical device submerged in water that you will connect to an electric outlet, you should **work under the supervision of a knowledgeable adult.**

Put a 6- or 7-oz Styrofoam cup in a glass or beaker. The glass will provide better support for the light, somewhat tippy Styrofoam.

Pour 100 g of *cold* water into the Styrofoam cup. The water should be cold—about 10°C (18°F) below room temperature—because the water will lose heat to the cooler air when its temperature rises above that of the surrounding air. By starting with the water below the temperature of the room, some heat will flow into the water during the first part of the heating process. This will compensate for the heat lost when the water temperature exceeds room temperature.

It is not necessary to weigh the water. Since 1.0 ml of water weighs 1.0 g, you can obtain 100 g of water by pouring 100 ml of cold water into the Styrofoam cup.

Place the unconnected immersion heater in the water along with a thermometer, as shown in Figure 15. **Never connect an immersion heater to an electrical outlet unless it is submerged in a liquid.** Make sure the thermometer is not touching the immersion heater. When the temperature stops changing, record the water's temperature. **Under adult supervision,** plug the immersion heater

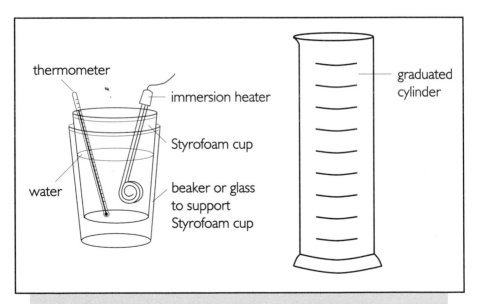

Figure 15. A thermometer and cold water can be used to find the heat delivered by an immersion heater in one minute.

into an electrical outlet. After exactly 30 seconds, disconnect the heater but leave it in the water so that all its heat will be transferred to the water. Stir the water and record its temperature when the thermometer reading remains steady.

What was the temperature change of the water (final temperature – initial temperature)? How much heat, in calories, did the heater provide during the 30 seconds it was connected? Remember, a calorie is the heat needed to raise the temperature of one gram of water by one degree Celsius. How many calories of heat are needed to raise the temperature of 100 g of water by one degree? By 10 degrees?

How much heat, in calories, will the heater deliver in one minute?

To check your prediction, repeat the experiment, but this time, leave the heater connected for exactly 60 seconds. What was the temperature change of the water this time? How much heat, in calories, did the heater deliver in one minute? Why might your measurement of the heat delivered not be exactly the same as your prediction? How is the heat delivered by the immersion heater related to the time it is connected to the electricity?

Repeat the experiment again, but this time use 200 g of cold water. You will need a larger (12-oz) Styrofoam cup for this experiment. Predict the temperature change that the water will undergo when the heater is again connected for exactly 60 seconds. Did the results confirm your prediction?

Predict the temperature change you will find when you heat 300 g of cold water for 60 seconds with the same heater. Predict the temperature change when you heat 300 g of cold water for two minutes with the same heater. Predict the temperature change when you heat 300 g of cold water for three minutes with the same heater.

How do your results compare with your predictions?

Based on your experiments, how much heat, in calories, does your immersion heater deliver per minute? Record this value. You will need it in the experiments that follow.

3-3
Measuring the Heat to Boil Water (Heat of Vaporization)

Things you will need:

- adult supervisor
- electric immersion heater
- 12-oz Styrofoam cups
- glass or beaker
- cold water
- graduated cylinder or metric measuring cup
- safety glasses
- oven gloves
- long sleeves
- thermometer with Celsius scale (–10°C to 110°C)
- electrical outlet
- stopwatch, clock, or watch with second hand
- pencil
- beaker
- scissors
- rigid-board insulation
- mineral wool insulation

Because this experiment requires the use of household electricity, it should be done under adult supervision.

It takes a considerable period of time to boil away a panful of water on a stove. A lot of heat has to flow into the water before all of it boils away. Of course, some of the heat is used to warm the water from its initial temperature to the boiling point (100°C, or 212°F), and some of the heat is needed to keep the water at the boiling temperature, because hot water loses heat to the cooler air that surrounds it.

You can estimate the heat of vaporization of water—the heat required to change one gram of liquid water to one gram of gaseous water at the boiling point—by using the immersion heater you used in the previous experiment to boil away some water.

From the previous experiment, you know how much heat the immersion heater delivers per minute. You will need that information for this experiment. Place a 12-oz Styrofoam cup in a glass or beaker. The glass will provide support for the less stable, lightweight Styrofoam. Pour 150 g (150 ml) of cold water into the insulated cup. For reasons of safety, wear safety glasses, oven gloves, and long

58

sleeves while doing this experiment. The water may spatter while boiling.

Place the unconnected immersion heater in the water along with a thermometer. **Never connect an immersion heater to an electrical outlet unless it is submerged in a liquid.** When the temperature of the water is steady, record the water's temperature. **Under adult supervision,** plug the immersion heater into an electrical outlet and leave it in the water for about 7 or 8 minutes. Once the water is boiling, record its temperature. Why might it boil at a temperature slightly below or above 100°C? After the allotted time, disconnect the heater. By then, a measurable amount of water should have boiled away.

Disconnect the heater at a known time and record the total time the heater was connected to electric power. Remove the heater and carefully pour the remaining hot water into a beaker or measuring cup and then into a graduated cylinder or metric measuring cup. What volume of water remains? How much water boiled away?

From the amount of heat the heater delivers per minute and the time it was connected, how can you calculate the total amount of heat supplied to the water by the heater? How much heat, in calories, was transferred to the water?

Some of the heat transferred to the water was used to warm the 150 g of water from its initial temperature to the boiling temperature. How much heat, in calories, was needed to raise the water from its initial temperature to its boiling temperature?

Assuming that the rest of the heat was used to change the water from liquid to gas—that is, to separate the molecules of water— how much heat was used to vaporize the water? How much heat was needed to vaporize one gram of water? What is the heat of vaporization of water according to this experiment?

To make a more accurate measurement of the heat of vaporization, you can provide better insulation and cover the water with another Styrofoam cup. Cut away the upper one third of the second

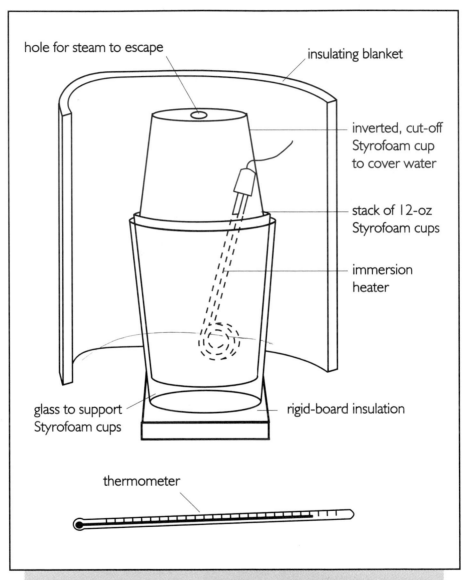

Figure 16. Using better insulation will help you obtain an accurate value for the heat of vaporization.

cup, and use a pencil to punch a hole in the bottom of that cup, from the inside to the outside. The hole will allow steam to escape. The cover will help insulate the cup and prevent spattering. If possible, use two or three stacked Styrofoam cups to hold the water, place the glass that supports the cups on a piece of rigid-board insulation, and surround the whole apparatus with a blanket of mineral wool insulation, such as that used to insulate the walls of houses (see Figure 16). Be sure you do not cover the top; the steam has to escape.

Using this better-insulated setup to reduce heat losses to the air and to prevent spattering, repeat the experiment. **Remember: Never connect an immersion heater to an electrical outlet unless it is submerged in a liquid. Under adult supervision,** connect the heater for exactly 8 minutes, measure how much of the 150 g of water remains after that time, and again determine the heat of vaporization for water.

A number of carefully conducted experiments show that the heat of vaporization for water is 540 calories per gram. How does this value compare with yours? By what percentage do they differ? Can you explain why your value might be different?

3-4*
Measuring the Heat to Melt Ice (Heat of Fusion)

As you know, it takes time for ice to melt. When the temperature of an ice-covered pond, or even an ice cube, reaches 0°C (32°F), the ice does not suddenly turn to water. A considerable amount of heat has to flow into the ice to make all of it melt. It takes time for this to happen. Ice melts slowly.

The heat of fusion for water is defined as the quantity of heat needed to melt one gram of ice. Now that you know how to measure heat, you can determine the heat of fusion. To begin, measure out 100 g (100 ml) of warm water at about 40°C (100°F) in a graduated cylinder or metric measuring cup. Pour the water into a 6- or 7-oz Styrofoam cup. Stir the water with a thermometer and record the initial temperature of the water.

Next, place an ice cube in the warm water. If there is a thin glaze of water on the ice cube, use a paper towel to dry the ice before adding it to the warm water.

Stir the water with the thermometer until the ice is completely melted. Then, determine and record the final temperature of the water.

What temperature change did the 100 g of water undergo as it transferred heat to the melting ice? How much heat, in calories, was lost by the 100 g of water?

To find out how much ice melted, pour the water back into the graduated cylinder. How much more than 100 ml was in the cup after the ice melted? How much ice melted?

Some of the heat lost by the warm water was used to melt the ice, but some of it was needed to warm the melted ice from its melting temperature (0°C, or 32°F) to the final temperature of the water and melted ice. How much heat was needed to warm the melted ice from 0°C to its final temperature? The rest of the heat must have been used to melt the ice. How much of the heat lost by the 100 g of warm water was used to melt the ice? What is the heat of fusion for ice according to your experiment; that is, how much heat was needed to melt one gram of ice?

A number of carefully conducted experiments show that the heat of fusion for ice is 80 calories per gram. How does this value compare with yours? By what percentage do they differ? Can you explain why your value might be different?

3-5*
Measuring Specific Heat

Because this experiment requires the use of household electricity, it should be done under adult supervision.

The specific heat of a substance is the heat required to raise the temperature of one gram of that substance by one degree Celsius. From that definition, you can see that the specific heat of water is 1.0 cal/g/°C. Most substances have a specific heat that is less than water's.

The specific heats of many liquids can be determined using

Things you will need:
- adult supervisor
- electric immersion heater
- cooking oil
- refrigerator
- graduated cylinder or metric measuring cup
- 6- or 7-oz Styrofoam cup
- glass or beaker
- thermometer (-10°C to 110°C)
- electrical outlet
- stopwatch, clock, or watch with second hand
- soap and warm water

the same immersion heater you used in the previous experiments. For example, you can find the specific heat of cooking oil easily.

In Experiment 3-2, you found the heat that your immersion heater delivers in one minute. You will need that value in this experiment. If you do not have it, go back and do that experiment before you start this one.

Place a bottle of cooking oil in the refrigerator for several hours before you begin this experiment. This will lower the temperature of the oil a few degrees below room temperature and compensate for the heat losses that will occur when the oil is heated above room temperature.

Since the density of cooking oil is approximately 0.90 g/ml, you will need to measure out 111 ml of cooking oil to obtain 100 g of the substance:

$$\frac{100 \text{ g}}{0.90 \text{ g/ml}} = 111 \text{ ml}$$

Measure the cooking oil in a graduated cylinder or metric measuring cup. Pour all of it into a 6- or 7-oz Styrofoam cup supported by a glass or beaker. Place the unconnected immersion heater in the cold oil along with a thermometer. **Never connect an immersion heater to an electrical outlet unless it is submerged in a liquid.** Make sure the thermometer is not touching the immersion heater. When the temperature stops changing, record the oil's temperature. **Under adult supervision,** plug the immersion heater into an electrical outlet. Continue to **hold the immersion heater so that it does not touch the sides of the cup.** Because **cooking oil is such a poor conductor of heat, the heater will melt a hole through the cup if it touches the Styrofoam.**

After exactly 30 seconds, disconnect the heater but leave it in the oil and use it to stir the liquid. When the temperature of the oil stops rising, record its final temperature. What was the temperature change of the oil (final temperature – initial temperature)?

From a previous experiment, you know how much heat, in calories, the heater provides per minute. How much heat, in calories, does it provide in 30 seconds? Since you know how much heat the immersion heater delivers in 30 seconds, you know how much heat, in calories, was delivered to the cooking oil.

Now, the specific heat of the cooking oil is the quantity of heat needed to raise the temperature of one gram of the oil by one degree Celsius. You know how much heat was needed to raise the temperature of 100 g of the oil through whatever temperature change you found and recorded. Suppose you found that the temperature of the oil rose from 10°C to 30°C, a temperature change of 20°C. If your heater delivers 1,200 calories in 30 seconds, then it delivered 12 calories per gram of oil, because

$$1{,}200 \text{ cal} \div 100 \text{ g} = 12 \text{ cal/g}$$

Each gram of oil underwent a temperature change of 20°C. Therefore, the specific heat of the oil, according to these data, would be

$$12 \text{ cal/g} \div 20°C = 0.60 \text{ cal/g/}°C$$

That is, 0.60 cal is required to raise the temperature of 1.0 g of cooking oil by 1.0°C.

Using your data, what is the specific heat of cooking oil?

Wash the immersion heater in warm soapy water before you put it away. If you would like to find the specific heat of other liquids such as ethylene glycol, the antifreeze used in car radiators, **check with your adult supervisor.**

3-6*
Finding Specific Heat by Mixing

Another way to find specific heat is to use the method of mixtures. A substance whose specific heat is unknown is thoroughly mixed with a substance whose specific heat is known, such as water, in a well-insulated container. If the two substances are at different temperatures, the warmer one will transfer heat to the cooler one until their temperatures are equal. Since the specific heat of one substance is known, the heat it gained or lost can be calculated:

heat gained or lost = mass of substance x temperature change x specific heat

Things you will need:
- graduated cylinder or metric measuring cup
- cooking oil
- 12-oz Styrofoam cups
- refrigerator
- thermometer (-10°C to 110°C)
- warm water (about 40°C or 100°F)
- adult supervisor
- safety glasses
- cooking pan
- stove or hot plate
- 6- or 7-oz Styrofoam cup
- steel washers (50g)
- string
- various metals, such as copper, lead, zinc, brass, bronze, or iron (50 g of each)

Since heat is a form of energy, and energy is never gained or lost, the heat gained or lost by the substance whose specific heat is known must have come from, or gone to, the other substance. Consequently, its specific heat can be calculated.

To see how this works, pour 100 g (111 ml) of cooking oil into a 12-oz Styrofoam cup. Place the cup in a refrigerator for several hours until it cools well below room temperature. After the temperature of the cooking oil reaches the temperature of the refrigerator, record its temperature, but leave it there while you prepare the water.

Pour 100 g (100 ml) of warm tap water at about 40°C (100°F) into another Styrofoam cup. Record the temperature of the water.

Then quickly remove the cooking oil from the refrigerator and pour the warm water into the cooking oil. Stir the two liquids thoroughly with the thermometer. Cooking oil does not dissolve in water, so you must keep stirring the two liquids until the temperature stops changing. Record the final temperature of the mixture.

From the data you have collected, you can find the specific heat of the cooking oil. Suppose, for example, your data look like those in the chart below.

Substance	Mass (g)	Initial temperature (°C)	Final temperature (°C)	Change in temperature (°C)
water	100	40	29	11
cooking oil	100	7	29	22

The heat lost by the water can be calculated easily:

$$100 \text{ g} \times 11°C = 1,100 \text{ cal}$$

Because energy is conserved, the heat gained by the cooking oil must be 1100 calories. The heat gained per gram of cooking oil was

$$1,100 \text{ cal} \div 100 \text{ g} = 11 \text{ cal/g}$$

Each gram of oil underwent a temperature change of 22°C; therefore, the specific heat of the oil, according to these data, would be

$$11 \text{ cal/g} \div 22°C = 0.5 \text{ cal/g/°C}$$

You can use this method to measure the specific heat of solids as well as liquids. For example, you could weigh out 50 g of steel washers and tie them together with a piece of string. Then, wearing safety glasses and **under adult supervision,** lower the washers into a pan of boiling water. As the temperature of the washers rises to 100°C, pour 50 g (50 ml) of cold tap water into a Styrofoam cup. Record the temperature of the boiling water and the cold tap water. *Quickly* remove the hot washers and put them into the cold water. Stir the water and record the final temperature.

The data can be used to find the specific heat of the washers or any other metal whose specific heat you wish to determine. You could, for example, find the specific heat of copper, lead, zinc, brass, bronze, iron, and (if you are rich) silver and gold.

4

Angles and Heights; Distances and Times

In this chapter you will see how angles can be measured and how these angles can be used to find angular distances in the sky and actual heights of real objects such as buildings and trees. You will also learn how measurements of distance and time enable us to determine speeds and velocities, and how velocities and times can provide the information needed to determine both distances and accelerations.

4-1*
Measuring Angles: An Astrolabe

An astrolabe is a device that can be used to measure angles in the sky and on the earth. You can build an astrolabe like the one shown in Figure 17 quite easily. Take a square sheet of cardboard about 30 cm (12 in) on a side. Use a protractor to mark off angles from 0 to 90 degrees as shown. Tape a drinking straw with a large diameter to the top of the cardboard. At the point where all the degree lines meet, make a small hole with a pin. Run one end of a length of thread about 45 cm (18 in) long through the pinhole. Tie the end

Things you will need:

- square sheet of cardboard about 30 cm (12 in) on a side
- protractor
- tape
- large drinking straw
- pin
- thread
- paper clip
- steel washer or nut, or fishing sinker
- a partner
- sheet of paper
- ruler
- sharp pencil

you have threaded through the hole to a paper clip on the unmarked side of the cardboard. The clip will keep the end of the thread in place. Tie the other end of the thread to a steel washer, a metal nut, or a fishing sinker. The weight will serve as a plumb line. It will always pull the thread vertically, toward the earth's center.

Once you have made your astrolabe, you can use it to measure the angular heights (the angle between the horizon and the object) of stars, planets, and the moon, as well as the actual heights of flag-poles, trees, and buildings. You might begin by measuring the angular height of the moon. The moon is easy to find and sight on through the straw.

Have a partner record the angle by observing the position of the string while you fix your sight on the moon through the straw. What is the angular height of the moon?

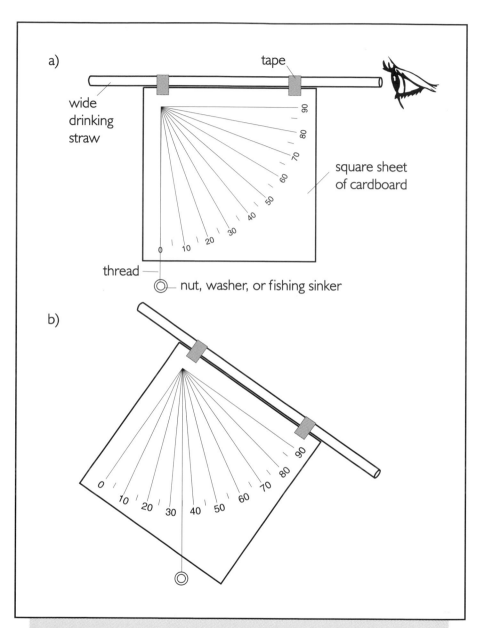

a)

tape

wide
drinking
straw

square sheet
of cardboard

90
80
70
60
50
40
30
20
10
0

thread

nut, washer, or fishing sinker

b)

0
10
20
30
40
50
60
70
80
90

Figure 17. a) An astrolabe can be made from a sheet of cardboard, thread, tape, a drinking straw, and steel washer. b) When an object is viewed through the straw, the string, which will be vertical, indicates the object's angular altitude in degrees. In the case shown, the altitude is 35 degrees.

Measure the angular height of the moon shortly after it rises and every hour thereafter, for as long as possible. How does the angle change as the moon moves across the sky? What is the largest angle you measured? Try it at different times of the year. At what time of year do you find the moon reaching its maximum angular height? What is that height?

Try to find the North Star (Polaris). If you cannot find it, ask someone familiar with the night sky to point it out to you. What is the angular height of Polaris? Does it change during the night?

Measure the angular heights of some other stars and planets. Do their angular heights change with time? How can you explain the constant angular height of Polaris?

If you travel, take your astrolabe with you. Use it to measure the angular height of Polaris at different latitudes. You will find that the angular altitude of Polaris is the same as the latitude at which you measure it. See if you can carefully draw some geometric diagrams to explain why the angular height of Polaris is the same as the latitude at which it is measured.

4-2*
The Ratio of Circumference to Diameter and a New Astrolabe

Things you will need:

• several different circular objects such as tin cans, bicycle wheels, coffee mugs, jars and lids, etc.

• ruler

• tape measure

• scissors

• file folder

• tape

• meterstick or yardstick

To measure the angular distance between stars or between any two distant objects that are separated horizontally, you can build a different kind of astrolabe, one that is based on the number of degrees in a circle. But first, take some time to consider circles.

The circle is an interesting shape. Unlike rectangles and triangles, the ratio of the perimeter (circumference) of a circle to its width (diameter) is always the same. To find out what that ratio is, find a number of different circular objects. You might include tin cans of different sizes, bicycle wheels, coffee mugs, jars and lids, etc. For the smaller objects, you can use a ruler or a tape measure to determine the diameter and circumference of each object, as shown in Figure 18a. Make your measurements carefully and accurately. Record the diameter and circumference of each circle in your notebook.

For larger objects, such as bicycle wheels, you can measure the diameter and then determine the circumference by marking the tire and a corresponding point on the ground. Roll the wheel through one full circumference until the mark on the tire again touches the ground (Figure 18b). Make a second mark on the ground beside the mark on the tire. Why will measuring the distance between the two marks on the ground give you the circumference of the wheel? Again, record the diameter and circumference of each circular object you measure.

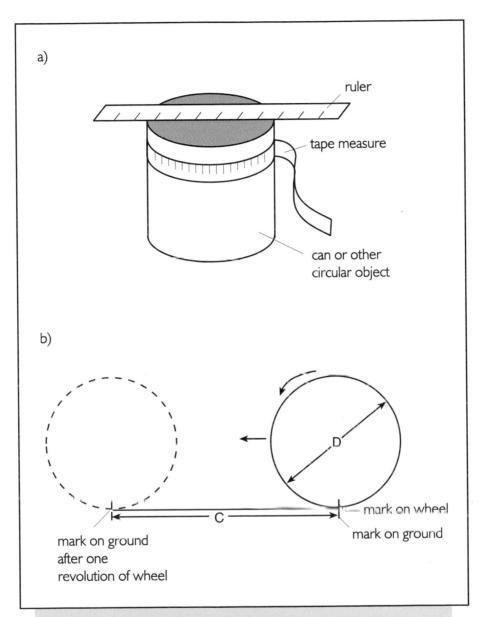

a)

ruler

tape measure

can or other
circular object

b)

D

mark on wheel

mark on ground

mark on ground
after one
revolution of wheel

C

Figure 18. a) The ratio of the circumference of a circle to its diameter for small circular objects can be found by direct measurement. b) Large objects, such as a bicycle wheel, can be rolled one revolution (turn) to find their circumference.

Now, for each circle whose circumference and corresponding diameter you measured, divide the circumference by the diameter and record the quotient. How do the quotients compare? The values of circumference divided by diameter that you calculated may differ slightly from each other, but it can be shown using more advanced mathematics that the ratio of the circumference of a circle to its diameter is always exactly the same. It is a number we call π (pi), a never-ending decimal that is approximately 3.1416.

Suppose you had a circle with a circumference of 360 cm. Because there are 360 degrees in a circle, radii ending at one-centimeter intervals along the circumference would form angles of one degree, as shown in Figure 19a. The diameter of such a circle would be

$$360 \text{ cm} \div \pi = 114.6 \text{ cm}$$

Therefore, the radius of the circle would be 57.3 cm. You can use this information to build an astrolabe that will enable you to measure the angular separation of stars and other distant objects.

Figure 19b shows how you can cut a 15 cm x 5 cm (6 in x 2 in) piece of manila file folder so that it has grooves 10 cm, 5 cm, 2 cm, and 1 cm wide. (Each groove is 1 cm high.) When the card is taped to a meterstick at a point 57.3 cm from one end (22 9/16 in from the end of a yardstick), the grooves provide angles of 10, 5, 2, and 1 degree when you place your eye at the end of the stick, as shown in Figure 19c.

Angular Distances Between Stars and Distant Objects

Use the astrolabe you have just made to measure (a) the angular distance between stars in the Big Dipper; (b) the angular distance between the Big Dipper and Polaris; and (c) the angular dimensions of various constellations. If you know the distance between two

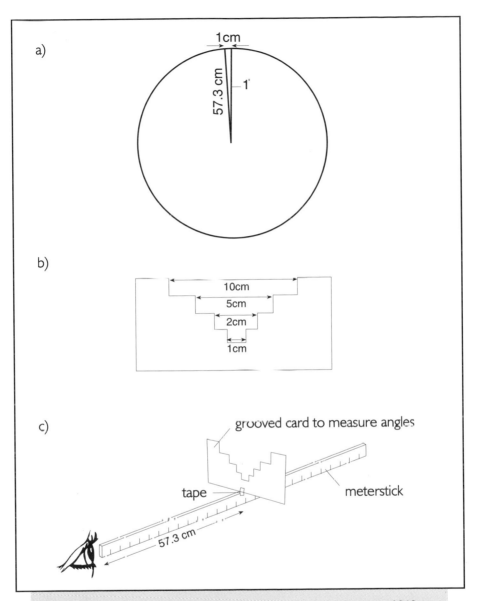

Figure 19. a) A circle with a radius of 57.3 cm has a circumference of 360 cm. Radii drawn to successive one-centimeter separations on the circumference will be one degree apart. b) A card with slots 10 cm, 5 cm, 2 cm, and 1 cm wide will correspond to angles of 10, 5, 2, and 1 degree when viewed from a distance of 57.3 cm. c) Taping the card 57.3 cm from the end of a meterstick will make an astrolabe that can be used to measure the angular separation of distant objects.

distant landmarks, how can you use your astrolabe to measure the distance from those landmarks to your eye?

Exploring on Your Own

In another piece of file folder, cut a square hole 10 cm on a side and tape it 57.3 cm from one end of a stick. When you view the night sky through this opening, you will see about 0.5 percent (1/200) of the total sky. To see why this is true, find the total area of a hemisphere (the sky's shape) with a radius of 57.3 cm. Remember, the surface area of a sphere is $4\pi r^2$. What is the surface area of a hemisphere with a radius of 57.3 cm? How can you use this instrument to estimate the number of stars visible in the night sky?

4-3*
Measuring Angles to Find Heights Through Scaled Drawings

You can use the astrolabe you made in Experiment 4-1 to measure the height of a flagpole, a tall building, a tall tree, a cliff, or any other tall object. Stand on a level surface at some convenient distance from the object whose height you wish to measure. Turn the astrolabe upward until you see the top of the tall

Things you will need:
- astrolabe made in Experiment 4-1
- a friend
- tall objects such as a flagpole, building, tree, cliff, etc.
- measuring tape
- paper
- ruler
- sharp pencil

object through the straw. Have a partner record the angle indicated by the weighted thread on your instrument. Then mark your position on the ground and use a measuring tape to find your distance, d, from the base of the object, as shown in Figure 20a. Finally, measure the height of your eye above the ground.

On a sheet of paper, make a scaled drawing (Figure 20b) of your measurements. You might, for example, let 1 cm of length on your drawing represent 1 m in your actual measurements. Use a ruler and sharp pencil to draw a horizontal line representing your distance, d, from the base of the object. At the end of the line, at the point that represents the place where your eye measured the angle, use a protractor to construct the angle you measured when you sighted on the top of the object. Draw a dotted vertical line representing the near side of the tall object at the other end of the line. Next, extend the angle you constructed until it meets the vertical dotted line. Use the scale drawing to find the height, h, of the tall object. Why must you add a height equal to the distance from your eye to the ground to find the actual height of the object?

Repeat this experiment on a number of different tall objects. If the actual height of an object is known, you can compare it with the

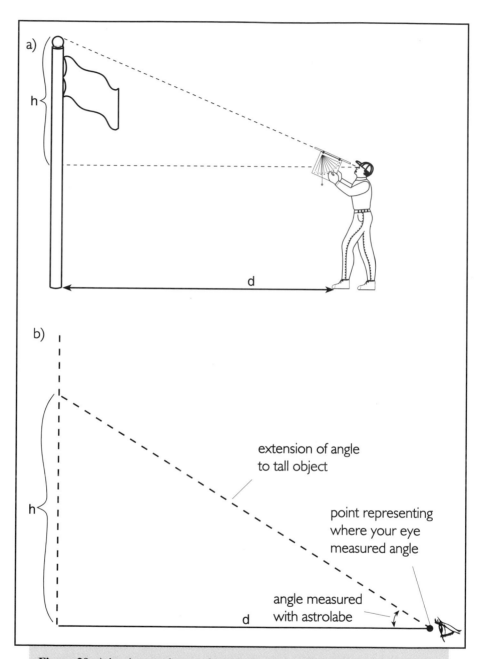

Figure 20. a) At a known distance from the base of a tall object, use your astrolabe to find the object's angular height. b) Make a scale drawing of the situation. In this drawing, 1.0 cm = 2.0 m.

height you determined. By what percentage does your measurement differ from the actual height?

Exploring on Your Own

Use your astrolabe to measure the height of trees in your neighborhood. Which kind of tree is on the average tallest?

How can you find the diameter of a tree trunk?

Do taller trees always have greater diameters than shorter trees?

4-4*
Distance, Time, and Velocity

The average velocity of a moving object can be found by dividing the total distance it travels by the time it takes to go that distance. For example, a car is driven from Boston, Massachusetts, to Hartford, Connecticut, a distance of 177 km (110 mi), in 2.0 hours. The car's average speed was

Things you will need:

- two partners
- marked football field
- stopwatch or watch with a second hand
- pencil and notebook
- graph paper

$$177 \text{ km} \div 2.0 \text{ h} = 89 \text{ kph, or } 110 \text{ mi} \div 2.0 \text{ h} = 55 \text{ mph}$$

Of course, the driver did not drive at a constant speed during the entire trip. She or he may have stopped for fuel, slowed down to avoid an accident, accelerated to pass a slow-moving truck, stopped to pay a toll, and so on. The calculation simply gives the average speed for the trip. To find a car's velocity at any moment, you can either watch the speedometer or measure the car's change in position over very small intervals of time.

Incidentally, velocity and speed are not the same. Speed is simply distance divided by time; velocity is speed in a particular direction. The value 40 kph is a speed; 40 kph due north is a velocity. Generally, we are interested in velocity, whether we know it or not, because we usually travel toward a destination that is located in a particular direction relative to our starting point.

Constant Speeds

You can find the velocity of someone walking. Have a friend walk at a steady pace from one goal line of a football field to the other, a distance of 100 yd (300 ft). At the moment your friend starts walking, start a stopwatch or note the position of the second hand on a watch. At each line marking 10 yd (30 ft), look at your watch to see

82

how much time has passed. Have another friend record the times in a notebook.

Record the data for several such walks in which the walker maintains a steady pace. One walk should be at a slow pace, a second somewhat faster, and a third at a normal pace. The data recorded by the author for two such walks are shown in Table 2. How do the data in the table compare with yours? Use your data to plot graphs of distance, in feet (ft), versus time, in seconds (s). (The author's graphs of his walks are shown in Figure 21. Both graphs are plotted on the same set of axes. How do they compare with yours?)

Table 2: Times recorded at ten-yard intervals for two walks from goal line to goal line along the sideline of a football field

Distance walked (yd)	Walk 1	Walk 2
	Time elapsed (s)	Time elapsed (s)
10	20.1	6.0
20	39.8	11.9
30	60.0	18.1
40	79.7	24.0
50	99.8	30.2
60	120.0	35.9
70	139.5	42.1
80	160.2	48.0
90	179.7	53.9
100	199.7	60.2

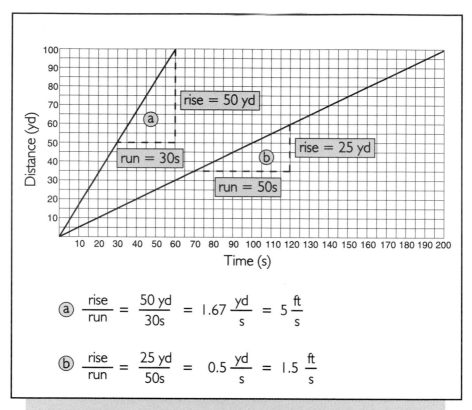

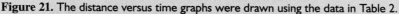

Figure 21. The distance versus time graphs were drawn using the data in Table 2.

The slope (rise ÷ run) of a distance-versus-time graph (see Figure 21) gives the speed of the moving object or person. What was the author's speed on each of his walks? What was your friend's speed on each of the walks he or she made? What additional information would you need to express the speeds as velocities?

Now that you know the speeds or velocities at which your friend walked, plot a graph of speed versus time for each walk. You can use the same set of axes for all your graphs. Figure 22 shows the velocity-versus-time graphs for the author's two walks. The speeds were obtained from the slopes of the graphs in Figure 21. Since those slopes were reasonably constant, the speed for each walk is shown to be constant. Because the speed is constant, the slope of

84

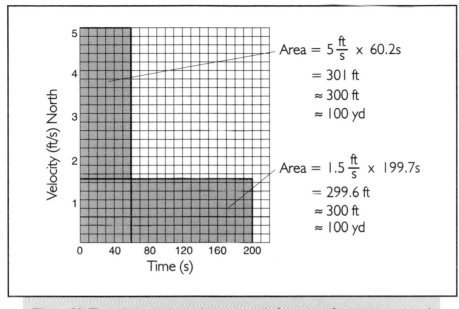

$$\text{Area} = 5\,\frac{\text{ft}}{\text{s}} \times 60.2\text{s}$$
$$= 301\text{ ft}$$
$$\approx 300\text{ ft}$$
$$\approx 100\text{ yd}$$

$$\text{Area} = 1.5\,\frac{\text{ft}}{\text{s}} \times 199.7\text{s}$$
$$= 299.6\text{ ft}$$
$$\approx 300\text{ ft}$$
$$\approx 100\text{ yd}$$

Figure 22. The velocity-time graphs were made from the information contained in the distance-time graphs in **Figure 21**.

these graphs is zero; there is no change in the velocity and, therefore, no acceleration.

Notice the shaded areas under the two graphs in Figure 22. As you can see, they form rectangles. The area of any rectangle is the product of its length and height. The area of the rectangle obtained for the slower walk in Figure 22 is 1.5 ft/s x 199.7 s, or 299.6 ft. The area of the rectangle obtained for the faster walk in Figure 22 is 5.0 ft/s x 60.2 s, or 301 ft.

You may find it strange to see that an area can represent a distance. However, it makes good sense mathematically, because the product of speed and time—the dimensions of the sides of the rectangles—is distance. You know that if you travel at a speed of 50 mph for 2 h you will go a distance of 100 mi (50 mph x 2 h = 100 mi), so it is reasonable to think of the area under a velocity-time graph as representing distance. In fact, there are many instances in which the area of a graph can represent something other than area

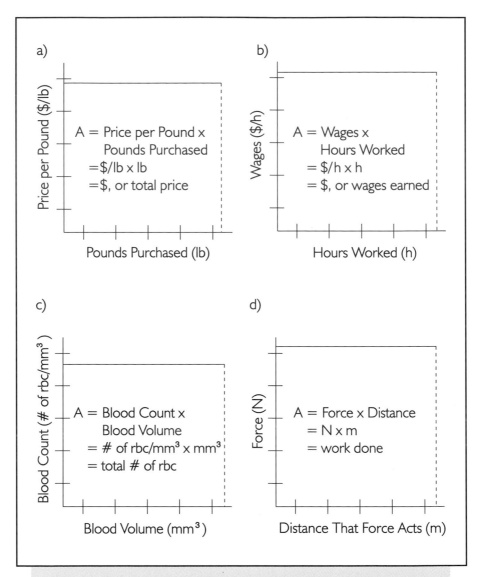

Figure 23. The area under a graph can represent many things other than a distance times a distance: a) area = total price; b) area = wages earned; c) area = total number of red blood cells in a person's blood; d) area = force x distance, which is the definition of work in physics.

in the sense of a length times a width. A few examples are given by the graphs shown in Figure 23.

Compare the areas under the speed-versus-time graphs for the walks that your friend made. What do you find? What is the total distance according to the area under the graph in each case? Can you explain why they are the same or nearly the same?

Exploring on Your Own

What is the cost of a can of your favorite soda? Plot a graph of cost versus the number of cans of soda you drink.

How can you use the velocity-versus-time graph for an object that is changing its velocity to find the acceleration of the object at any moment in time?

A ball is thrown straight up into the air. Plot a graph of a) the ball's velocity versus time; b) the ball's acceleration versus time.

4-5*
Nonconstant Speeds: Making and Interpreting Graphs

The concept of distance as the area under a velocity-time graph can extend to graphs in which the speed is not constant. Figure 24 shows the speed-versus-time graph for a train that moved at different speeds over a period of several minutes. The total distance the train traveled can still be found by determining the area under the graph. The task is

Things you will need:

- Figure 24
- car or bus with a speedometer and odometer
- driver for car or bus
- stopwatch or watch with second hand
- pad and pencil
- graph paper
- a friend

somewhat complicated because the area under the graph is not a simple rectangle. Part of it is rectangular, part is triangular, and part is irregular. The parts must be added to find the total distance. The job is easy for the rectangular and triangular portions. To find the total area for the irregular parts, you will have to find the area of one of the squares on the graph paper and count the total number of squares in the irregular part. Where only part of a square is under the graph, you will have to estimate the fraction that is. What do you estimate was the total distance traveled by the train during the period shown in the graph?

A Real-Life Study of Speed versus Time

You can make a real-life speed-versus-time graph. Sit where you can read the speedometer of a car or bus in which you are traveling. Before the vehicle begins to move, record the odometer reading and a speed reading of 0 at time 0. At the moment you start to move, have a friend note the time. The same friend can indicate 10-second intervals to you by simply saying "Time" every 10 seconds. You can record the reading on the speedometer after each 10-second interval

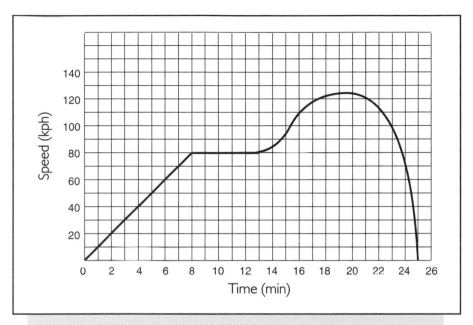

Figure 24. The speed-versus-time graph for a train in which the speed varies and in which changes in speed are not always constant.

for as long as the trip continues or until you decide to stop. At the moment the trip ends or whenever you decide to stop recording data, record the new odometer reading.

From the data you have collected, plot a speed–time graph. Then determine the area under the graph. Remember, 10 seconds is 1/6 of a minute or 1/360 of an hour. According to your graph, how far did the vehicle travel between odometer readings? How does the value you determined from your graph compare with the difference between the actual odometer readings?

Exploring on Your Own

On a highway that has mile markers, record the time as you pass each marker. After leaving the highway, use your data to plot a graph of average speed versus time. Compare the distance traveled according to your graph with the distance traveled according to the mile markers.

4-6*
Constant Acceleration

Things you will need:

- two straight boards 1.2 m (4 ft) long
- level floor
- short board
- golf ball or large marble
- marking pen
- meterstick or yardstick
- graph paper
- stopwatch (optional)

Find two straight boards 1.2 m (4 ft) long. Place the boards side by side on a level floor. Separate the two boards a bit to make a groove between them. Then raise one end of the boards slightly by placing a short board under them, as shown in Figure 25a. Next, place a golf ball or a large marble at the raised end of the boards and release it. Does the sphere appear to accelerate (speed up) as it rolls down the incline? If the ball does not roll or rolls at what seems to be a nearly constant speed, raise the ends of the boards a little by moving the short board farther from the raised ends (closer to the middle) of the boards.

Draw a line near the raised end of the boards to serve as a starting line. Next, mark the boards at 25 cm, 50 cm, 75 cm, and 100 cm (10 in, 20 in, 30 in, 40 in) from the starting line, as shown in the drawing. Release the ball from the starting line. Does it appear to accelerate as it rolls past the lines on the board?

Constant acceleration means that an object's speed increases at a steady rate; that is, its speed increases by the same amount during successive equal intervals of time. There is an easy way to tell whether or not the ball has a constant acceleration. Figure 25b is a graph showing constant acceleration. The slope of the graph (rise ÷ run) is constant, and the slope gives the acceleration because it is the change in velocity divided by the change in time.

You know that the area under the graph of a speed-versus-time graph gives the distance traveled. The graph in Figure 25b has been divided into a number of small triangles. Each triangle, as you can

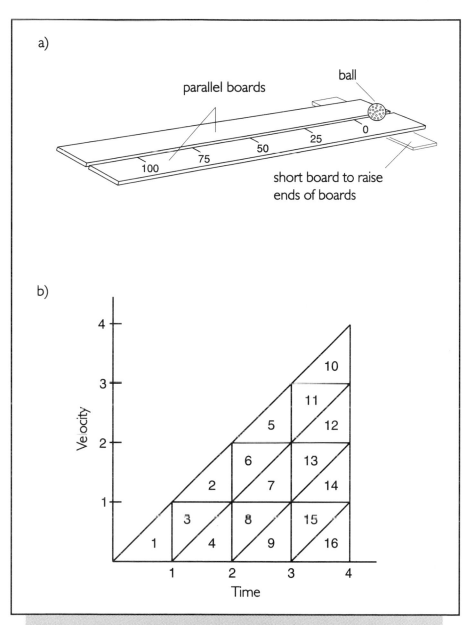

Figure 25. a) Does a ball accelerate as it rolls down an incline? You can find out by measuring the time a ball takes to roll different distances. b) An object with constant acceleration travels distances that are proportional to the square of the time traveled.

see, has the same area as the first triangle, which represents the distance traveled during the first second. By counting the triangles, you can see that the total distance traveled after 2 seconds is equal to 4 small triangles, or 4 times the distance traveled during the first second. After 3 seconds, the total distance traveled is equal to the area of 9 small triangles, or 9 times the distance traveled during the first second. Similarly, the distance traveled after 4 seconds is 16 times the distance traveled during the first second. Table 3 summarizes the information given in the graph and gives the total distance traveled after equal intervals of time.

Table 3: The distances traveled after equal time intervals by an object that has constant acceleration

Time	Time squared (T^2)	Total distance
1 unit	1 unit^2	1 unit
2 units	4 units^2	4 units
3 units	9 units^2	9 units
4 units	16 units^2	16 units

As you can see from the graph and the table, an object with constant acceleration travels distances that are proportional to the squares of the travel times.

To see if the ball rolls down the incline you made with constant acceleration, you can measure the time it takes to roll 25 cm, 50 cm, 75 cm, and 100 cm (10 in, 20 in, 30 in, 40 in). You can use a stopwatch to measure time if you have one. If not, you can count to five (one, two, three, four, five) as fast as you can. You will find it takes just about one second. You can then use your fast count repeated several times to find the time required for the ball to roll different distances. Record distance and time for each of the distances the ball rolls. Repeat your measurements several times to be sure the results are consistent.

How do the distances the ball rolls compare with the squares of the times required to roll those distances? You may be able to compare these two quantities more easily if you plot a graph of distance rolled versus the square of the time to roll those distances. Is the graph a straight line? If it is, what does it tell you about the acceleration? If it is not a straight line, what does it tell you?

Exploring on Your Own

Design and carry out an experiment to find out whether a falling object has a constant acceleration.

5

Math and Sports

Athletics provides a rich reservoir of subjects for investigations that require mathematics. In this chapter you will have a chance to look at a few of the places where sports and mathematics intersect. We begin with a look at comparative speeds on base paths and tracks.

5-1*
Running Bases versus Straight-line Dashes

"Cool Papa" Bell played in the professional Negro Leagues that existed before baseball was integrated in 1947 when Jackie Robinson appeared as a Brooklyn Dodger. Cool Papa was known for his speed. It was reported that he could make it around the bases, all 360 feet of

Things you will need:
- regulation baseball field with bases
- measuring tape
- stopwatch or watch with second hand
- pencil
- paper
- a partner

them, in less than 13 seconds. If you do not think that is quite a feat, try it yourself. Ask someone to use a stopwatch, or a watch with a second hand, to measure the time it takes you to round the bases pretending you are trying for an inside-the-park home run. (Use a regulation field with 90-foot base paths, not a Little League field.) Record the time it took you to run the bases. Then, if your friend is interested, measure the time it takes him or her to run around the bases as fast as possible.

How does your time to round the bases compare with Cool Papa Bell's time? Express Bell's time compared to yours as a fraction. Compare the times as a decimal fraction. Compare his time as a percentage of yours.

What was Cool Papa's average speed, in feet per second, in rounding the bases? What was your average speed? How do they compare? Should they be in the same ratio (fraction) as the times? Explain your answer.

Do you think you could run at a faster speed if you did not have to change direction the way you do in rounding bases? To find out, use a long measuring tape to measure out a straight-line distance of 360 ft (120 yd). Have your friend measure the time it takes you to run this straight-line distance. Record the time and calculate your speed, in feet per second, in running this 120-yd dash. What is the ratio of your time to run the dash to the time to run the bases? What is the ratio of the speeds for these two runs?

Perhaps the increase in time to run bases as compared with dashes is related to the extra distance you have to run because you cannot really run along straight lines when rounding the bases. To find out, have someone watch your path as you round the bases while running as fast as you can. If the diamond has dirt base paths, you will be able to see your footprints, which will make it easy to mark your path. Once you know the path you follow in running the bases, use a long measuring tape to find the total distance you ran while traveling around them. How far did you actually run? Record that distance. How much farther than 360 ft did you actually run in rounding the base paths?

Using the distance you actually ran and the time it took you, calculate your average speed in running around the bases. How much faster was your actual speed than the speed you calculated when you assumed a distance of 360 ft?

Compare your actual speed with the speed at which you ran the 120-yd dash. Does the added distance involved in running the bases account for your reduced speed in running bases as compared with a dash? Or do you think changing direction is a factor as well? Which do you think is more responsible for the reduced speed in running bases, the actual distance of the run or the changes in direction? What evidence can you offer to support your position?

In 1996, the world record for the 100-m dash was set by Donovan Bailey at the Summer Olympics. Bailey ran the dash in 9.84 s. One meter is equal to 3.28 ft. What was Bailey's average speed, in feet per second, for this dash? How does his speed compare with Cool Papa Bell's in running the bases, assuming Bell followed the same actual path that you did?

Assume that Cool Papa Bell's speed in running the bases was the same fraction of the speed he could achieve in running a 120-yd dash as yours was. At what speed would Bell have run the dash? How would Bell have fared in a race against Bailey?

Although Jesse Owens, who held the Olympic record for the 100-m dash with a time of 10.3 s in 1936, often traveled with Negro League teams and ran races against fans and sometimes horses in pregame festivities, he would not race Cool Papa Bell. How did Owens's average speed in the 100-m dash compare with Bell's in running the bases?

Earlier you calculated Bell's speed in running the 120-yd dash assuming the ratio of his dash speed to base-running speed was the same as yours. If that calculation gave Bell's correct average dash speed, how would he have fared in a race against Jesse Owens?

Exploring on Your Own

From an almanac you can obtain information about track length and winning times for famous horse races such as the Kentucky Derby. Use that information to determine the average speed of fast-running horses. How does it compare with the speeds of fast-running humans? How does it compare with the speeds of fast-skating humans?

5-2*
Bouncing Balls

When a ball bounces from a surface, part of its energy of motion (kinetic energy) is changed to elastic energy as the materials in the ball are squeezed together (compressed) during the collision with the surface. As the elastic materials return to their normal shape during the rebound, some of the elastic energy is changed back to the

Things you will need:
- meterstick or yardstick
- clothespin
- various balls such as a rubber ball, a Styrofoam ball, a Super Ball, a ball made of modeling clay, as well as sports balls such as those used for baseball, soccer, tennis, lacrosse, basketball, squash, handball, golf, etc.

kinetic energy of the ball. The rest appears as thermal energy (heat). A similar thing happens when people engage in bungee jumping (a sport the author does not recommend).

If all the kinetic energy is restored after a collision, the collision is said to be elastic. But only atomic collisions are truly elastic. If all the kinetic energy is lost, the collision is said to be inelastic.

Measuring Bounciness

Hold a ball so that the bottom of the ball is level with the top of a meterstick or yardstick. Release the ball and watch closely to see how high it bounces after it hits the floor. Use a clothespin to mark the point on the meterstick to which the bottom of the ball bounced. Repeat the experiment several times to be sure you have marked the height correctly.

To what height did the ball bounce? To what fraction of its original height did it rise?

Repeat the experiment, using other balls. You might include a rubber ball, a Styrofoam ball, a Super Ball, and a ball made from modeling clay, as well as balls used in various sports such as baseball, soccer, tennis, lacrosse, basketball, squash, handball, and golf.

Use the percentage of its original height that the ball acquires after bouncing once as a measure of its bounciness. For example, if a ball falls from a height of 1.0 m (100 cm) and rises to a height of 70 cm on its first bounce, its bounciness is

$$70 \text{ cm} \div 100 \text{ cm} = 0.70 = 70 \text{ percent}$$

How does the bounciness of each ball compare with the others'?

A Super Ball is probably the bounciest ball. Which is the least bouncy? Which is the bounciest sports ball? The least bouncy sports ball?

You might try dropping the balls on various surfaces such as wood, concrete, tile, brick, grass, or dirt. How does the surface affect a ball's bounciness? Which surface seems to provide the highest bounces? Devise a way to mathematically rate surfaces for providing bounce.

Exploring on Your Own

You measured the percentage of the height that a ball achieves on its first bounce. How high do you think each ball will bounce on its second bounce? On its third bounce? Pick one ball and determine its bounce height after one, two, three, and perhaps more bounces. If you have trouble doing this, simply measure the height of the first bounce. Then drop the ball from the height to which it bounced and measure the height to which it returns. For example, if the ball, after falling from 1.0 m, bounces to a height of 70 cm, release it from a height of 70 cm and mark the height of its next bounce. If it rises to 50 cm after this bounce, release it from 50 cm to determine the height of its third bounce.

Did you find any elastic collisions in the experiments you did? Did you find any inelastic collisions?

5-3*
Curveballs: Ratios and Proportions

Although it takes skill and practice to become a good curveball pitcher, you can make a beach ball or a Styrofoam ball curve quite easily. To see such a ball curve, launch it forward, using both hands. Just before you release the ball, put spin on it by

Things you will need:

- beach ball or Styrofoam ball
- data in Table 4
- graph paper
- pencil
- ruler

pushing one hand forward as you pull the other hand back. If you put a clockwise spin on the ball, which way does it curve? If you put a counterclockwise spin on the ball, which way does it curve?

For years, despite the testimony and repeated whiffs of frustrated batters, many people believed that curveballs thrown by baseball pitchers were optical illusions. The matter should have been settled in 1870 when pitcher Freddy Goldsmith threw a spinning baseball at three carefully aligned vertical rods. The path followed by Goldsmith's curveball is shown in Figure 26. Despite the clear proof provided by Goldsmith and the theoretical explanation provided by Sir Isaac Newton more than three hundred years ago, the illusion argument persisted.

A series of carefully designed experiments to examine the factors involved in making a baseball curve was carried out by physicist Lyman J. Briggs about forty years ago. In his experiments, Briggs allowed a baseball to fall 6 ft across the center of a wind tunnel. He chose to drop the ball 6 ft because it takes a ball about 0.6 second to fall through this height. The time for a pitched ball to travel from the pitcher's mound to home plate is also approximately 0.6 second. Briggs used a machine to spin the ball clockwise or counterclockwise about a vertical axis before it was released. As it fell, air flowed past the spinning ball at speeds comparable to the air speeds that would move across a baseball thrown horizontally

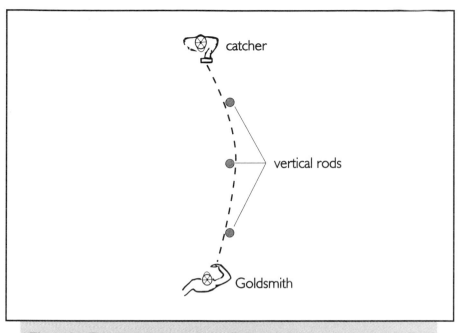

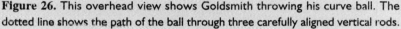

Figure 26. This overhead view shows Goldsmith throwing his curve ball. The dotted line shows the path of the ball through three carefully aligned vertical rods.

by a pitcher. After all, the speed of the air relative to the ball is the same regardless of whether it is the ball or the air that is moving.

Briggs found that if the ball was released without any spin, it would be blown slightly backward by the wind, but it was not deflected either to the right or to the left. A spinning ball, however, was always deflected to one side or the other as it fell.

Table 4 shows how the deflections were affected by both spin and wind speed. The spin rates of the balls just before they were dropped are given in revolutions per second (rev/s); the wind speeds are given in feet per second (ft/s), meters per second (m/s), and miles per hour (mph); and the deflections of the ball (the distance it was displaced from a straight-line fall) are given in inches (in) and meters (m). The wind speeds are comparable to the speeds at which pitchers throw balls toward home plate, and the spin rates are similar to those a pitcher might put on a ball by snapping his wrist as he throws.

Ratios and Proportions

Is the deflection of the ball proportional to its rate of spin? When the ratio between the quantities of two variables is constant, we say the variables are proportional. Another way of saying this is when the quantity of one variable is equal to the quantity of another

Table 4: The lateral deflection of a spinning baseball during a six-foot drop across a wind tunnel at various wind speeds and rates of spin (Data are from an article by Lyman J. Briggs, *American Journal of Physics*, vol. 27, p. 591, 1959.)

Ball's rate of spin (rev/s)	Wind speed*			Deflection	
	(ft/s)	(m/s)	(mph)	(in)	(m)
20	75	22.9	51	6.1	0.150
20	100	30.5	68	11.7	0.297
20	125	38.1	85	17.8	0.452
20	150	45.7	102	26.0	0.660
30	75	22.9	51	9.4	0.239
30	100	30.5	68	17.5	0.445
30	125	38.1	85	25.8	0.655

*Speeds and deflections are abbreviated: ft/s = feet per second; m/s = meters per second; mph = miles per hour; in = inches; m = meter.

variable multiplied by some constant number, the two quantities are proportional to each other. For example, if apples cost $1.00 per pound (lb), the price of the apples you might buy is given by

Price = $1.00/lb x weight of apples in pounds

Or using our first and equivalent definition

$$\frac{\$1.00}{1\ lb} = \frac{\$2.00}{2\ lb} = \frac{\$3.00}{3\ lb} = \ \ldots$$

We say the price of apples is proportional to the weight of apples purchased.

Similarly, the circumference of a circle is proportional to its diameter because the circumference of any circle equals its diameter times π (pi), or stated another way, for all circles,

circumference ÷ diameter = π

If two variables are proportional, the ratio of their quantities will be constant. In the two examples used in the previous paragraph, you can see that

$$\frac{Price}{weight\ of\ apples} = \$1.00 \quad and \quad \frac{Circumference}{diameter} = \pi$$

Another way, often used by scientists, to find out if two variables are proportional is to plot a graph. The quantities for one variable are plotted on the vertical axis, and the corresponding quantities for the other variable are plotted on the horizontal axis. Graphs of the two examples used above are shown in Figure 27. The slope of the graphs (the rise over the run), as seen in Figure 27, must be the ratio of the quantities of the two variables.

Deflection and Rate of Spin

To find out if a baseball's deflection is proportional to its rate of spin, the wind speed must be constant. If both the wind speed and the spin were allowed to change, you would have no way of

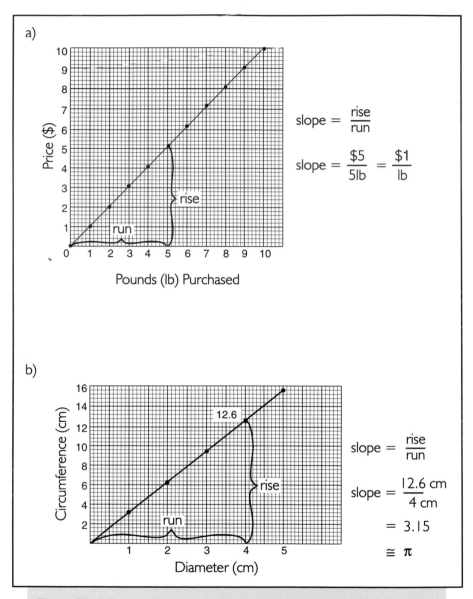

Figure 27. a) A graph of price (of apples) versus pounds purchased shows that the two variables are proportional. The slope gives the constant ratio. b) This graph shows that the circumference of a circle is proportional to its diameter. The slope is equal to π. There is always some error involved in measuring real circles, so the slope may not be exactly equal to π. A geometric theorem shows that in the perfect world of pure mathematics circumference ÷ diameter = π.

knowing whether the deflection was caused by the rate of spin, the wind speed, or both. Fortunately, the table provides two different rates of spin at several different wind speeds. To find out if the deflection of the ball is proportional to spin, compare the ratio

$$\frac{\text{rate of spin}}{\text{deflection}}$$

for spins of 20 and 30 rev/s at a constant wind speed of 22.9 m/s. Repeat the calculations for rate of spin/deflection for wind speeds of 30.5 m/s. Repeat them again for wind speeds of 38.1 m/s. Are the ratios for rate of spin to deflection reasonably constant for any fixed wind speed? Remember, these are the ratios of measurements, and in making measurements there is always some error. A rough estimate of the errors in measuring spin and deflection is 5 percent for each. Consequently, the error that might be expected in their ratios is 10 percent. Are the ratios all within 10 percent of one another for a fixed wind speed? If they are, the rate of spin and deflection are probably proportional.

Deflection and Wind Speed (or Speed that a Baseball Travels Through Air)

To see whether or not there is a relationship between the deflection of the ball and wind speed—the rate at which air moves by the ball (or the speed at which the pitcher throws the ball)—the spin rate must be constant. Why?

Choose 20 rev/s as a fixed rate of spin. This time, to find out whether or not deflection is proportional to wind speed (or ball speed through still air), plot a graph of deflection versus wind speed. What does this graph tell you about the relationship between deflection and wind speed?

On a second graph, plot deflection versus wind speed *squared* when the spin rate is kept at 20 rev/s. (Do not forget to plot the origin—zero deflection for zero spin.) What do you find? Can you draw a reasonably good straight line through the points on your

105

graph? (Remember, there was probably some error in making the measurements.) What does this tell you about the relationship between the ball's deflection and the square of the wind (or ball) speed? Is the deflection of the ball proportional to the square of the wind (or ball) speed? How can you tell?

What do you predict the graph will look like if you plot deflection versus wind speed squared when the spin rate is fixed at 30 rev/s? Plot the data on the same set of axes. Does the graph look the way you predicted it would?

What do these graphs tell you about the relationship between the deflection of the ball and the square of the speed of the air moving past it?

Combining Relationships

You have seen that the deflection of a baseball is proportional to both its rate of spin and to the square of its speed through the air (wind speed in the experiment). You might guess that the deflection of a baseball will be proportional to the product of the rate of spin and the wind speed squared. After all, the area of a rectangle is proportional to both its length and its width. Doubling either will double the rectangle's area. The area of a rectangle is also proportional to the product of its length and width (area = length x width).

To see if the deflection of a baseball is proportional to the product of its rate of spin and the square of its speed through air (wind speed in the experiment), you can plot a graph. Plot the product: rate of spin x (wind speed)^2 on the vertical axis and the corresponding deflection in meters (m) on the horizontal axis for each set of data in Table 4 (p. 102).

Can you draw a reasonably straight line through all the points in your graph? What do you conclude? Is the deflection of a baseball proportional to the product of its rate of spin and its speed squared? If it is, what is the value of the following ratio?

$$\frac{\text{rate of spin (rev/s)} \times \text{speed squared (m}^2\text{/s}^2)}{\text{deflection (m)}}$$

In other words, what is the slope of the graph?

Using the Equation

Using the equation you have found, how much would a ball be deflected during a period of approximately 0.6 second if its spin rate is 25 rev/s and its speed is 40 m/s?

If it is deflected 0.40 m and its speed, as determined by a radar gun, is 85 mph, what was its rate of spin?

Exploring on Your Own

Pitchers find that in throwing a curveball from the pitcher's mound to home plate, the ball's deflection can be increased by giving it more spin. However, they claim that the ball's deflection is about the same whether they throw the ball at 60 mph or at 90 mph. Why does a ball, given a fixed rate of spin, curve by the same amount between the pitcher's mound and home plate regardless of its speed? Hint: Consider the number of turns the ball will make in its journey from the pitcher's mound to home plate, which is 60.5 ft (18.4 m) away.

In Table 4 (p. 102), the rates of spin are given in revolutions per second. What are the rates of spin in degrees per second?

List of Suppliers

The following companies supply the materials that may be needed for science fair projects:

Carolina Biological Supply Co.
2700 York Road
Burlington, NC 27215
(800) 334-5551; http://www.carolina.com

Central Scientific Co. (CENCO)
3300 CENCO Parkway
Franklin Park, IL 60131
(800) 262-3626; http://www.cenconet.com

Connecticut Valley Biological Supply Co., Inc.
82 Valley Road, Box 326
Southampton, MA 01073
(800) 628-7748

Delta Education
P.O. Box 915
Hudson, NH 03051-0915
(800) 258-1302

Edmund Scientific Co.
101 East Gloucester Pike
Barrington, NJ 08007
(609) 547-3488

Fisher Science Education
485 S. Frontage Road
Burr Ridge, IL 60521
(800) 955-4663; http://www.fisheredu.com

Frey Scientific
100 Paragon Parkway
Mansfield, OH 44905
(800) 225-3739

Nasco-Modesto
P.O. Box 3837
Modesto, CA 95352-3837
(800) 558-9595; http://www.nasco.com

Nasco Science
P.O. Box 901
Fort Atkinson, WI 53538-0901
(800) 558-9595

Sargent-Welch/VWR Scientific
911 Commerce Court
Buffalo Grove, IL 60089-2375
(800) 727-4368; http://www.SargentWelch.com

Science Kit & Boreal Laboratories
777 East Park Drive
Tonawanda, NY 14150-6782
(800) 828-7777; http://sciencekit.com

Wards Natural Science Establishment, Inc.
5100 West Henrietta Road
P.O. Box 92912
Rochester, NY 14692-9012
(800) 962-2660; http://www.wardsci.com

Further Reading

Books

Adler, Irving. *Mathematics*. New York: Doubleday, 1990.

Bernstein, Bob. *Mathemactivities*. Columbus, Ohio: Good Apple, 1991.

Burns, Marilyn. *Math for Smarty Pants*. New York: Little, Brown & Co., 1982.

Gardner, Robert, and Edward A. Shore. *Math & Society: Reading Life in Numbers*. Danbury, Conn.: Franklin Watts, Inc., 1995.

————. *Math in Science and Nature: Finding Patterns in the World Around Us*. New York: Franklin Watts, Inc., 1994.

Miller, Don. *Mental Math & Estimation*. White Plains, N.Y.: Cuisenaire Company of America, Inc., 1992.

Sharp, Richard M., and Seymour Metzner. *The Sneaky Square and 113 Other Math Activities for Kids*. Blue Ridge Summit, Pa.: TAB, 1990.

Smoothey, Marion. *Number Patterns*. Tarrytown, N.Y.: Marshall Cavendish, 1992.

Stwertka, Albert. *Recent Revolutions in Mathematics*. New York: Franklin Watts, Inc., 1987.

Thomas, David A. *Math Projects in the Computer Age*. Danbury, Conn.: Franklin Watts, Inc., 1995.

Internet Addresses

Morano, David. "Experimental Science Projects: An Introductory Level Guide" *Cyber-Fair*. May 27, 1995. <http://wwww.isd77.k12.mn.us/resources/cf/SciProjIntro.html> (August 6, 1998).

Swarthmore College. "The Math Forum." June 16, 1998. <http://forum.swarthmore.edu> (August 6, 1998).

Index